G000097572

THE
WINE LOVER'S
—GUIDE TO—
The Rhône
and South-East France

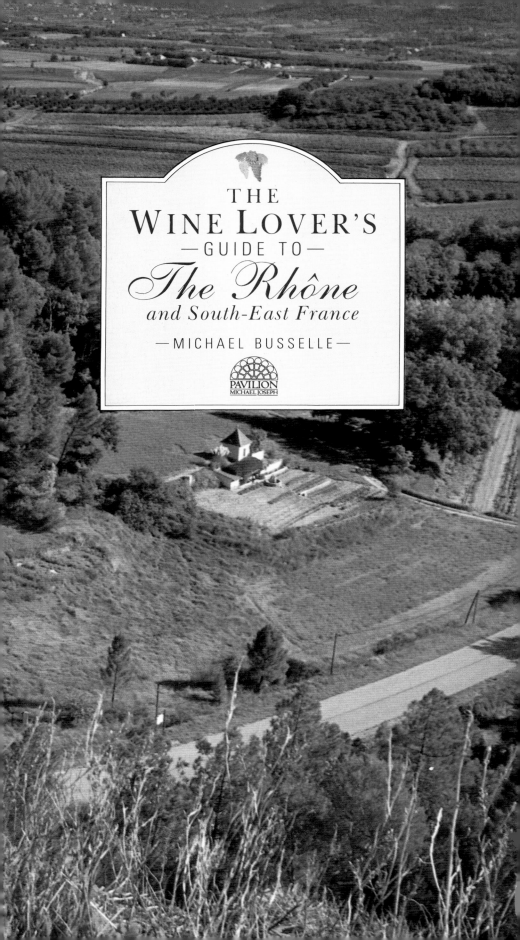

THE
WINE LOVER'S
—GUIDE TO—
The Rhône
and South-East France

—MICHAEL BUSSELLE—

PAVILION
MICHAEL JOSEPH

First published in Great Britain in 1990 by
PAVILION BOOKS LIMITED
196 Shaftesbury Avenue, London WC2H 8JL
in association with Michael Joseph Limited
27 Wrights Lane, Kensington, London W8 5TZ

Photographs and wine tours text
copyright © Michael Busselle 1986
Wine-buying guides compiled by Graham Chidgey &
Lorne Mackillop copyright © Pavilion Books 1986
Other text by Ned Halley copyright © Pavilion Books 1990

Series Editor Ned Halley
Designed by Bridgewater Design Ltd
Map by Lorraine Harrison

All rights reserved. No part of this publication may be
reproduced, stored in a retrieval system, or transmitted, in
any form or by any means, electronic, mechanical,
photocopying, recording or otherwise, without the prior
permission of the copyright holder.

A CIP catalogue record for this book is available from the
British Library

ISBN 1-85145-242-7

10 9 8 7 6 5 4 3 2 1

Printed and bound in Spain by Graficas Estella

*Previous pages: The view over the landscape of the
Vaucluse from the clifftop village of Roussillon*

Contents

Introduction

The Abbaye de Hautecombe on the shores of Lac du Bourget seen from a viewpoint on the D 944

*T*HEIR WINEMAKING ACTIVITIES ASIDE, the common thread running through the regions of Savoie, the Rhône, Languedoc and Provence is that they all serve France as popular holiday resorts. Each of these regions owes much of the fame of its wines to the tourists who have enjoyed them *en vacances* and spread the word throughout France, and beyond.

Abroad, it must be said, Savoie is distinctly better known for its skiing than it is for its delectable white wines. Likewise, Provence remains a mecca more for sun-worshippers and film-stargazers than for seekers after that region's unquestionably newsworthy *vins rouges*, *blancs* and *rosés*.

The Rhône Valley is more familiar territory. Everyone knows about Côtes du Rhône, and Châteauneuf-du-Pape must be one of the most recognisable wine village names of them all. Similarly, while the regional name Languedoc might mean little to most travellers, some of its *appellation contrôlée* districts are immediately recognisable – Corbières, Fitou, Minervois.

But the Rhône and Languedoc, both producers of wine on a vast scale, have countless appellations making wines that remain largely unknown outside their immediate locality. It is among these vineyards that exciting new aromas and flavours are to be found – and the extraordinary talents of winemakers in the warm South, many of them new to the region, discovered.

Among the 'Case for Tasting' features that appear after each tour in this book, the reader will see some wines that are likely to be familiar, and some that will probably be rather less so. The Languedoc wine Mas de Daumas Gassac is a good example of a name that may ring few bells. It ranks as a mere *vin de pays de l'Hérault* and is made at a farmhouse remotely positioned at

Aniane on Languedoc's eastern edge. But the wine has been described in France's leading wine guide, *Gault-Millau*, as 'the Château Lafite of Languedoc'. It is, indeed, one of the greatest wines made in France – and very well worth a detour, for wine-lovers.

Serendipitous discoveries such as Daumas Gassac are the landmarks of wine tours of these beautiful regions, while the prevailing theme is that of relishing the consistently high standard to which southern French wines are now being made. The raisiny, stewed-tasting reds and tired, flat whites that made so much Mediterranean wine rightly notorious in the past are disappearing fast as production levels fall and investment in new technology rises. Take, for example, the large Languedoc district of Corbières. For generations, 100,000 acres of vineyards here produced a veritable wine lake of *vin ordinaire* by wringing the last drop of juice from every over-ripened grape. Then in the 1970s, wine consumption in the locality started to fall – reflecting

A shady country lane in the valley of the River Argens near the wine town of Les Arcs

an overall decline in France from the 1970 figure of 110 litres per head per year to something like 80 litres now. Winemakers, for all the support the EEC might offer them, simply could not sell their production. Many vineyards were abandoned, but others determined to look to new markets, abroad, where demand for good quality wines was growing.

Today, the *vignerons* who moved over to making those quality wines are prospering from the benefits of planting more classic vine varieties such as Cinsault and Carignan, Grenache and Syrah, and by installing the latest winemaking equipment complete with cooling devices to cope with the very hot southern conditions prevailing at harvest time. In December 1985, Corbières was rewarded with full *appellation contrôlée* status for its vineyards

An ancient shuttered shop front in the small village of Azille in the Minervois

(now down to under 60,000 acres) – with all the strict quality control that the designation implies.

It is the same story all over southern France, of reducing production, and soaring standards – of delicious discoveries to be made in a region not so long ago mocked for the coarseness of its wine.

More good news from the region: the wines remain, for the moment, very reasonably priced. Single-estate wines of real quality can be bought from growers throughout all four regions described in this book at under 20FF a bottle. These regions are, in fact, among the most suitable in France for buying wine direct – as many of the types on offer will be unavailable abroad, and are very much cheaper than you will find them at the few specialized merchants who do ship them.

Growers in the Savoie, Languedoc and Provence – and to a lesser extent in the Rhône, where the bigger names have agents abroad – are anxious to sell their wine direct to the public, because they lack retail outlets. And as they are not generally competing with merchants, the winemakers sell their wares at 'farm gate' prices – rather than at prices hiked up in order not to undercut the retailers they supply.

It goes without saying, of course, that you should always taste any unfamiliar wine before you buy it. *Dégustation* tends to be offered wherever *vente directe* is advertized.

As always when buying wine *in situ*, it is important to look after it on the way home. At all costs, avoid leaving wine exposed to direct sunlight in your car, as one good overheating – a likely occurrence in the south of France – can ruin it entirely. It makes sense, therefore, if you have a load of wine on board, to park the car in the shade as much as possible.

*The remote and peaceful Lac de Thuile in the mountains to the south east
of Chambery*

Skiers buying a box or two of finest Savoie to bring home from a winter holiday on the slopes would likewise be sensible not to leave wine overnight in the car if there is likely to be a frost. Should the wine freeze, it will force the corks out of the bottles and be spoiled.

In every region, don't forget to note any wine particularly enjoyed with a restaurant meal. Write down the name of the estate and the grower – you can look these up in the booklets provided by local *comités* (associations of winemakers) at tourist offices in the provincial towns, and visit the estate to buy the wine direct. It's the way many long-established wine merchants discover new wines – and a happy method for less knowledgeable customers of making friends among the *vignerons*, who like nothing better than to be sought out by an appreciative enthusiast.

Savoie

*Above: Vineyards in the Savoie near the wine village of St Badolph to
the south of Chambery*
*Left: Savoyard vineyards near the village of Apremont with Mont
Granier in the background*
*Following pages: Springtime near Correns where vineyards and olive
groves dominate the landscape*

*I*T IS A PITY that so little attention is paid to the wines of Savoie,
because the vineyards are extensive, the wines distinctive and the
countryside most alluring. The wine-growing area of Savoie is concentrated
mainly in four regions: on the southern shores of Lake Geneva, along the
banks of the Upper Rhône, in the hills around the Lac du Bourget and in the
valleys to the south of Chambéry.

THE WINES

The wines of Savoie are mainly white (often *pétillant*), with some red and little
rosé, and are produced from a variety of grape types. The main appellations
are Seyssel, Crépy and Roussette.

Roussette de Savoie is a white wine made from a mixture of the Altesse and
Mondeuse grape types, which are grown around the towns of Frangy and
Seyssel. A little further to the south, a red wine is made from the Mondeuse,
Gamay and Pinot Noir grapes in a region called the Chautagne: the villages
where the main production is centred are Ruffieux, Chindrieux, Motz and
Serrières-en-Chautagne. A red wine made exclusively from the Mondeuse
grape is found in the villages of Arbin, Cruet and St Jean-de-la-Porte to the
south of Chambéry.

Vin de Savoie, a white wine from the Chasselas grape, is made in the
vineyards beside Lake Geneva. The appellation Crépy is also from this area,
as are the Marignan, Ripaille and Ayze appellations.

The bridge spanning the Rhône which divides the town of Seyssel

THE CUISINE

Dairy products are a strong feature of Savoie cooking. Cows' milk is used for *Tomme de Savoie* and *Comté* cheeses – large, flat cylinders of firm creamy-coloured cheese with a deliciously nutty flavour and a satisfying texture. *Bleu de Gex* is a blue-veined cheese known as *fromage persillé* because it has a similar marbled appearance to the *jambon persillé* of Burgundy. *Reblochon* is a creamy but firm yellow cheese, while *Saint-Marcellin* is milder, softer and ivory coloured. Cream and cheese are also used in cooking. *Pommes de terre dauphinoise* is a wickedly rich dish of thinly sliced potatoes baked slowly in a shallow dish with butter and cream. In *pommes de terre à la savoyarde* meat stock is used instead of cream and grated *Comté* cheese is added.

THE ROUTE DES VINS *Michelin maps 74 and 77*

The Savoie wine route is not a true circuit, although if you use either Aix-les-Bains or Chambéry as a base you can make two separate circuits taking in the entire route. Most of the route I suggest is signposted; it goes from north to south with the town of Frangy (which is very close to exit 11 on the Autoroute A 40) as the starting point. Frangy is a lively small town astride the N 508 in the valley of the River Usses, and is known for its appellation Roussette de Savoie. Take a small road, the D 310, out of the town towards the hamlet of Desingy (this part of the route is not signposted). The quiet country lane leads through a peaceful, hilly landscape of vineyards and cornfields, woods and meadows. From here continue along the D 31 to Clermont, a village set on the hillside with views towards the Alps, where you can visit the large thirteenth-century château. The route now continues along the D 57 through Droisy and then descends into the valley of the Rhône. The next stop is the little town of Seyssel, which is bisected by the river and famed

Maize drying in the eaves of a farmhouse in the village of Ruffieux is a common sight in the Savoie

for its Roussette de Savoie; it received its appellation in 1930 – late recognition for a town mentioned in eleventh-century records for its wine growing. *Méthode champenoise* white wine is also made here from Altesse (or Roussette) and Molette grapes.

Leaving Seyssel, the wine road continues beside the Rhône along the D 981 for a few kilometres until it meets the D 56, a small road that climbs up away from the river through vineyards towards the wine village of Motz. Continue through the hamlet of Chevignay to Ruffieux, where there is a *Cave Co-opérative* run by the Chautagne producers; there is another one in the neighbouring village, Serrières-en-Chautagne, beside the main road. A worthwhile short detour from Ruffieux takes you up a narrow winding road to the summit of Mont Clergeon, where you can look out over the Rhône Valley to some wonderful views of the snow-capped Alps to the east.

The next village, Chindrieux, is another commune within the Chautagne appellation; it is immediately to the north of the Lac du Bourget, in marsh-like terrain with brooks, slender trees and reed beds. The Route des Vins now follows the course of the Canal de Savières to Portout, a little village on the canal's bank. Leave the wine route here and follow the D 914, which winds round the side of the mountain above the lake: you will be rewarded with frequent dramatic glimpses of the blue-green lake far below, through dense woods. From the terrace of the café high in the hills you can see the lake and the Abbaye de Hautecombe far below on its shore: you can reach the abbey via a small road. It was built in the twelfth century by Cluniac monks but was heavily restored in the eighteenth and nineteenth centuries, in a somewhat extravagant style. The lakeside road now joins the main road. Turn off for the Col du Chat and begin to retrace your path along the wine route to the north of the lake. When you reach the top of the Col du Chat, the

A private château near the wine village of Billième in the countryside to the west of Lac du Bourget

Route des Vins follows a small road, the D 210, leading off to the right to the wine villages of Monthoux and Billième. The small villages here are quiet and undistinguished but have a rugged charm, the crumbling stone walls of the ancient houses and farms in strange contrast to the gleaming stacks of shrink-wrapped, virgin wine bottles awaiting use. The vineyards cling to the steep hillsides and there are frequent signs along the road, particularly in Billième, inviting you to stop and sample the local wines. The road descends now to the valley floor towards Lucey and the meadows of maize.

The Route des Vins continues along by the river on the D 921 to the village of Chanaz. Like its neighbour, Portout is situated beside the Canal de Savières and has a number of waterside restaurants and cafés. Take the main road, the D 991, along the eastern shore of the Lac du Bourget to the small but important wine-growing community around Brison-St Innocent. The village is, in fact, a residential suburb of Aix-les-Bains and the vineyards are cultivated between the gardens of the smart villas: the local climate is ideal.

There are no vineyards of significance now until you reach those south of Chambéry; to get there it is easiest to take the N 201 into the centre of the town. It would be a pity, however, not to linger a while in the elegant resort of

*Vineyards near the wine village of St Pierre-d'Albigny which overlooks
the valley of the River Isere*

Aix-lex-Bains. It has a long tree-lined lakeside promenade with cafés and
restaurants. All the usual seaside facilities are available here, from
sunbathing on the beach to windsurfing, swimming and boating, and the
modern thermal establishment is renowned for the treatment of rheumatism
and sciatica.

Jean-Jacques Rousseau lived at Chambéry for a while, and you can visit
Les Charmettes, the house he stayed in and described in his *Confessions*; it is
set in a quiet wooded hillside on the edge of the town. The wine route is
signposted again from the suburb of Barberaz along the D 201, a quiet road
which leads through the wine villages that nestle below the peak of Mont
Granier. The two appellations in this region are the white wines of Apremont
and Abîmes; the five communes of St Badolph, les Marches, Myans,
Apremont and Chapareillan are the centres of production. There are many
places where you can taste and buy the local wines and visitors are welcomed
at the *caves*.

The appeal of these wine villages, small, rather haphazard collections of
old stone houses and farms criss-crossed by narrow streets, lies mainly in the
wines they make and their beautiful mountain settings: it is worth taking one
of the many small roads that climb up into the vineyards above the villages,
from where there are stunning views of the distant valley of the Isère and the
mountains beyond. To enjoy the mountain scenery to the full you should also
make a detour to the top of the very dramatic Col du Granier. You get to it via
a narrow road that literally hugs its way around the side of the mountain
providing a constant display of staggering views over the sheer side to the
valley below and distant Chambéry.

From les Marches the Route des Vins crosses the Autoroute A 41 and the
main road, the N 90, to the town of Montmélian. There is a large *Cave*

*An old farmhouse among the vineyards in the countryside near Jongieux
to the west of Lac du Bourget*

Co-opérative here where you can taste and buy a variety of Savoie wines, including Mondeuse. The next stops are the wine villages of Arbin and Cruet, known for their red Mondeuse. The road follows the Isère Valley, climbing higher as it nears the villages of St Jean-de-la-Porte, St Pierre-d'Albigny, Miolans and Fréterive, the latter marking the limit of the wine route. The silvery Isère shimmers below you and the dramatic snow-capped peaks of the Massif de la Vanoise are clearly visible in the distance. An essential small detour here is to the Château de Miolans, perched high up on the hill; a small road climbs up to it.

If you retrace your steps to Cruet another narrow road, the D 11, winds up through the vineyards to the secluded lake of Thuile, an oval of limpid blue-green water surrounded by gently sloping meadows and ringed with reeds. From here there is a gentle drive through a series of small valleys back to the wine villages of Chignin and finally St Jeoire-Prieuré on the main road (the N 6), which will take you back into Chambéry or south to Grenoble and beyond.

The vineyards beside Lake Geneva are quite small in area and are concentrated around the towns of Evian, Thonon and Douvaine. Vin de Savoie is to be found at Ripaille and Marignan and the appellation Crépy in the communes of Douvaine, Loisin and Ballaison. I have not included these vineyards in the wine tour because they are not very extensive and are rather cut off from the rest of the wine-growing region. However it is worth making a small detour to taste these distinctive wines, and you will be made very welcome at the *caves*. One of particular interest is the Tour de Marignan, where there are fascinating ancient cellars in a fortified house dating back to the eleventh century. Not far from Lake Geneva are the appellations Marignan and Ayez in the valley of the Arve near the town of Bonneville.

A Case for Tasting

THE LIVELY DRY WHITES and many other wines made in Savoie are not widely known outside France. But as visitors to this popular skiing region know well, Savoie wines are a delight to discover.

CHIGNIN-BERGERON

The Bergeron grape makes some of the best white *Vin de Savoie*, particularly when cultivated at Chignin. André Quenard's Côteau de Torméry vineyard there produces a fine example at 40FF – pale but very well flavoured, with that distinctive slight sparkle of good Savoie wine.

MONTMÉLIAN

The *Co-opérative de Vente des Vins Fins de Savoie* at Montmélian – one of the ten villages that can append their names to the appellation – produces 24 different Savoies, all of good standard and at low prices. At under 20FF this clean dry white from Montmélian itself is an excellent example.

APREMONT

Apremont is one of ten villages entitled to attach their names to the *Vin de Savoie* appellation. This wine from the co-operative in Apremont, Le Vigneron Savoyard, is a typically light, crisp and lively white, and good value at 25FF.

ROUSSETTE DE SAVOIE

This appellation is for white wines made from the Altesse grape – known locally as Roussette. The wines have a golden hue, sweet and sometimes musky smell and lovely grapey-spicy flavour. Noël Dupasquier justifiably enthuses about the 'aromas of honey, almonds and truffles' that characterize his wine.

MARIGNAN

Marignan is a hamlet in the far north of Savoie where Bernard Canelli-Suchet makes splendid dry whites at what he claims is the oldest winery in the region – dating back to the eleventh century. The *perlant naturel* on the label refers to the wine's slight natural sparkle.

MONDEUSE

Noël Dupasquier makes consistently fine red wine from the Mondeuse grape. A sweet, plummy aroma and complex, lingering flavour mark the wine in good vintages. Pleasant to drink young – price is only about 20FF – but will also develop into a smooth, satisfying wine after a few years in bottle.

GAMAY ROSÉ

The grape more usually associated with Beaujolais grows in the Savoie with mixed success. Pierre Boniface of Les Rocailles makes a well-coloured, slurpably fruity pink wine of real character – to drink young, and preferably well chilled. He also makes a decent red Gamay.

VIN DE PAYS D'ALLOBROGIE

Good dry white wine at an everyday price – under 10FF – from the co-operative at Montmélian. This is humble *vin de table*, so not entitled to the Savoie *appellation contrôlée* – but the co-operative labels it with the unmistakable Savoie shield to dispel any doubts about the wine's origin.

ROUSSETTE DE SEYSSEL

Deep golden wine from the Altesse grape, with a highly distinctive aroma of violets. It is rather acidic in youth, but evolves after a couple of years in bottle into a fine dry wine that goes especially well with food. Varichon & Clerc is very much the dominant wine producer in Seyssel.

SEYSSEL VIN MOUSSEUX

Varichon & Clerc's sparkling Seyssel wines are the only part of Savoie's production to achieve export success on any scale. This dry, and very well made *brut* wine is sold abroad under various names – Carte Blanche and Le Duc among them. Try also the firm's delicious Royal Seyssel sparkler.

CRÉPY

Crépy is an *appellation contrôlée* district in its own right, producing excellent dry white wines which are light in body, but packed with fruity flavour – and with the characteristic *pétillance* of Savoie. Fichard's wine is among the best, and reasonable value at under 30FF.

BUGEY BRUT

Not a sparkling wine well known outside the region as the Seyssels are, Bugey Brut is nevertheless delicious and good value at 30FF. Very dry, but with an attractive, fruity bouquet, and lively, persistent bubbles. Made by the 'Champagne method' by Le Caveau Bugiste.

The Rhône

Above: An ancient Grenache vine in the Vaucluse vineyards near Gordes
Left: Modernised production methods mean that traditional wine-
making equipment like this is now used only for decoration

RUNNING SOUTH from Lyon – between the Savoie Alps to the East and the Massif Central to the West – towards the sprawling estuary beyond Avignon where it spills into the Mediterranean, the powerful Rhône River traverses a wide variety of landscape, from ruggedly dramatic, steep-sided valleys to flatter pastoral farm and meadowland. For over 200 kilometres, the banks of the Rhône are lined with vineyards, some teetering on precarious terraces high above the river, and others spread flat and wide as far as the eye can see. This is a region of great wines – of deep reds such as Châteauneuf-du-Pape and the rare 'Côte Rôtie', of Tavel and Lirac, two of the best rosés in the world, and the lovely spicy white wines of Condrieu and Château Grillet. The range is as enormous as the landscape is dramatic.

THE WINES

The 138 communes which make up the Rhône region produce a rich variety of wine, in terms of both quality and character. Some wines are made in quantities so small that a bottle almost becomes a collector's item. Others are produced on such a vast scale that huge machines are needed to harvest the grapes and the wine co-operatives look like oil refineries. The colour of the wines range from the deepest blood red through delicate pink to the palest gold. So, 'Côtes du Rhône' covers a huge variety of wines.

The *appellation contrôlée* wines within the department of the Rhône are: Côtes du Rhône (red, white and rosé); Côtes du Rhône-Rhône (red and white); Condrieu (white); Côte Rôtie (red); Côtes du Rhône-Loire (red and white);

Vineyards near the village of Beaumes-de-Venise on the slopes of the Dentelles de Montmirail

Château-Grillet (white); Côtes du Rhône-Ardèche (red and white); Cornas (red); Saint-Péray (white; *mousseux* as well as still); Côtes du Rhône-Drôme (red and white); Crozes-Hermitage (red and white); Saint-Joseph (red and white); Hermitage (red and white); Vin de Paille (white); Die (white sparkling): Tavel (rosé); Châteauneuf-du-Pape (red and white); Côtes du Rhône-Gigondas (red, white and rosé); Côtes du Rhône-Cairanne (red, white and rosé); Côtes du Rhône-Laudun (red, white and rosé); Côtes du Rhône-Chusclan (rosé); Côtes du Rhône-Vacqueyras (red, white and rosé) Côtes du Rhône-Vinsobres (red, white and rosé); Rasteau (red, white and rosé dessert wines and *rancio*); Beaumes de Venise (red wines and white dessert wines) and Lirac (red, white and rosé). In addition there are *marcs* and brandies and a number of VDQS wines.

THE CUISINE

The restaurants in Lyon are magnificent – they are owned and run by the most famous chefs in France. This city in the north of the Rhône region is renowned for all kinds of sausages, for its *quenelles* (fish balls) made of pike, for its tripe and chicken dishes and for sweets such as acacia-blossom fritters. Further south, the food takes on a distinctive southern character: the flavours are stronger, more garlic and olive oil are used. Perhaps the speciality of the southern Rhône area is the *bouillabaisse*, the great fish stew of Marseilles. There are many versions but they all should include a mixture of firm, white-fleshed fish, olive oil, garlic and onions, with saffron added for flavour and colour. Then there are the *daubes*, hearty stews of lamb or beef cooked slowly with wine, garlic and tomatoes and seasoned with aromatic herbs.

Pieds et paquets are sausage-like parcels of lambs' trotters and tripe stuffed with bacon, garlic and herbs and cooked in white wine. For those with a sweet tooth, the world-famous Montélimar nougat is not to be missed.

THE ROUTE DES VINS
Michelin maps 73, 74, 77, 80 and 81

Just 30 kilometres south of Lyon is Vienne, the starting point for the wine tour down the Rhône. The main wine road is the N 86, which follows the course of the river for about 70 kilometres. The first village on the Route des Vins is Ampuis, which produces the rare Côte Rôtie, a full-bodied, deep red wine that benefits considerably from ageing. The hillsides here rise sharply from

Ripening Grenache grapes in vineyards near Tavel in the southern Rhône
Following pages: Vineyards on the slopes of the Dentelles de Montmirail near the wine village of Gigondas

the river, almost like cliffs, and the vines are grown on narrow terraces, many of which date from Roman times. Ampuis itself was founded in 600BC by the Phoenicians. The Syrah grapes grown on these steep slopes, which face south west, are bathed in sunshine all day long, hence the name Côte Rôtie (literally, 'roasted slope'). A tiny road, the D 615, twists its way up the hillside behind the village and from it you get an excellent view over the terraced slopes to the Rhône far below.

The wines produced in the next two villages, Condrieu and Château-Grillet, in contrast, are heavily scented whites made from the Viognier grape. Both these wines are produced in very small quantities – Château-Grillet is the smallest appellation in France, with only about 3 hectares of vineyards – and consequently appeal as much for their rarity and snob value as for their character and quality. One place you can try them is at the two-star Beau Rivage restaurant which overlooks the Rhône at Condrieu.

There are no vineyards of interest now until Tournon. Across the river from here you can see a huge granite rock towering above the town of Tain-l'Hermitage, named after a knight crusader who 'retired' here and made wine. Its vineyards of Hermitage and Crozes-Hermitage produce a strong and full-bodied red wine from Syrah grapes which seem to thrive in the rough, rocky soil.

At Tain you could make a detour and follow a signposted route that takes you around the wine-growing communities of la Roche de Glun, Pont-de-l'Isère, Beaumont-Monteux, Chanos-Curson Mercurol, Crozes-Hermitage, Larnage, Serves, Erôme, Gervans and then back to Tain. It is not all vineyards. There are rich, flat meadows beside the river where a wide variety of fruit and vegetables is grown. In a layby outside Mercurol I met a man with

The old town of Pont-St Esprit seen from the bridge spanning the Rhône after which it is named

*Vineyards in the valley of the River Argens near Taradeau to the south
west of Draguignan*

a huge, black, greasy machine called an *alambic* (a still); it looked like an ancient traction engine and had a Heath Robinson air about it. He told me that he spent three months of the year towing it around the local communes and converting apples, plums and pears into *eau de vie*. On a good day he could produce up to 500 litres, he said. I tasted a sample of his work – and it was fiery indeed. He showed me, with some pride, a picture of a beautiful copper and brass still on cart-wheels. He used it until fairly recently, but is keeping it safe now. It's his pension, he explained wrily.

Once back at Tain, you cross to the west bank of the Rhône, where the N 86 continues through a succession of small wine-growing villages: St-Joseph, Cornas and St Péray, where red and white wines are made; St Péray also produces a sparkling white wine. There is a scenic detour at Cornas, up a small road that climbs towards St Romain de Lerps, where there is a ruined tower. You can return to the N 86 either by doubling back a little via the village of Plats and taking the D 219 into Mauves, or by turning left on the D 287 and driving down into St Péray.

These villages mark the limit of the northern Rhône vineyards and now it is some 90 kilometres before you reach the next wine areas. However, there are a number of detours off the N 86 which will make this an interesting journey. La Voulte is a fascinating old village perched on a rock topped by a sixteenth-century chapel. Further south, in one of the most beautiful spots in

An ancient village house in the southern Rhône

the Rhône Valley, is the village of Rochemaure. There is a fortified gate at each end of the centre of the village. If you stop to explore the ruins of the feudal castle here you will see that there is a split in the rock upon which it is built.

The N 86 continues south through the towns of Viviers and Bourg-St-Andeol to what is virtually the gateway of the southern Côtes du Rhône, Pont-St Esprit. This old market town is dramatically situated beside the torrential Rhône, its waters swollen by the confluence with the powerful Ardèche just to the north. The town is named after its thirteenth-century bridge, built by the Frères Pontifs, which spans the river. From here you can explore the southern Rhône vineyards and the wild and majestic gorges of the Ardèche, which lie a little to the west.

The Route des Vins now goes in three different directions. Crossing to the east bank you can follow the route from just outside Bollène towards the village of Ste-Cécile-les-Vignes. Here the terrain is flat and the vines stretch towards the horizon like a patterned green carpet. Although there is a maze of small roads criss-crossing the vineyards and leading to innumerable small villages, the Routes des Vines is extremely well signposted – so much so that you can virtually ignore the map and simply follow the signs to a succession of fascinating places. At Suze-la-Rousse, for example, there is a university of wine based in a vast château which towers above the small town, and many of the villages, including Bouchet, Cairanne and Roaix, have old fortifications, abbeys, châteaux and often wonderful views from their hill-top settings.

As you travel further to the east a range of jagged mountains begins to loom in the distance. These are the Dentelles de Montmirail; at their foot is

Gigondas. It is a handsome mountain village and produces a wonderful full-bodied, deep red wine from the Grenache, Mourvèdre and Syrah grapes that grow here. There is a small road that climbs up and through the mountain giving spectacular views towards the western Cévennes ranges and Mont Ventoux to the east. A little north of Gigondas is Séguret, one of the many little hill-top villages in the area but perhaps more self-conscious than most, having been taken up – and renovated – chiefly by wealthy Parisians.

A little further along the southern edge of the Dentelles de Montmirail are the wine villages of Vacqueyras and Beaumes-de-Venise. They both make good red wines, while Beaumes-de-Venise is famed for its heady Muscat, a rich, naturally sweet white wine which chilled can be served as an *apéritif* or more regularly with a dessert. A complete circuit of the Dentelles de Montmirail can be made by continuing round towards Malaucène and Vaison-la-Romaine.

Alternatively you can follow the signs for the Côtes du Ventoux from Malaucène. This route leads south through wonderfully scenic countryside, where the vineyards are mingled with lavender fields and the mountains are always in sight. Just outside the small walled village of Caromb is a *Cave Co-opérative* which also houses a small wine museum. You could stay overnight here in a little hôtel called Le Beffroi, which also has a restaurant. Bédouin and Flassan are two villages worth visiting; the latter is a very evocative

An ancient portable wine press decorating the entrance to the cave coopérative *of Caromb in the foothills of Mont Ventoux*

The pretty medieval village of La Roque-sur-Ceze to the south west of Pont-St Esprit

example of a Provençal village with its orangey-pink stone and red-tiled houses perched high above the surrounding countryside.

Continue through the village of Villes-sur-Auzon and then westwards again via Mormoiron and Mazan to Carpentras, a bustling market town, the medieval capital of the region until Pope Clement V decided that Avignon was more convenient. From here you can follow a circuit of the more southerly

wine-growing villages. Of particular interest on this route are the hilltop
towns of Venasque and Roussillon, one of the most superbly sited villages in
Provence, its ochre and red houses set on the brink of a sheer, rust-coloured
cliff. From the village there are breathtaking panoramas over the Côtes du
Ventoux. Nearby, close to Gordes, is the ancient Village des Bories, made up
of curious conical houses built from flat stones and perfectly preserved.

Heading towards Avignon, make a detour via the wine town of Bédarrides
to Châteauneuf-du-Pape. All that is left of its papal château is a ruined wall

*A truck-load of grapes ready to be taken to the wine press near the village
of Lirac in the southern Rhône*

and tower. Up to thirteen different grape varieties are used in the making of
the village's famous rich red wine; they grow in a soil studded with round
white stones, like small boulders, which store the heat of the sun and release it
at night.

Of course you must stop in Avignon. Its medieval Palais des Papes was the
home of seven French popes; it is an imposing fortress-like structure with a
strong Mediterranean character. The famous Pont d'Avignon has only 4 of its
22 arches now, but retains its chapel. Avignon holds a music and theatre
festival in high summer every year and it attracts some world-famous
performers.

The circuit on the western side of the Rhône starts from Villeneuve-lès-
Avignon, a suburb of the city. There are two routes. You can travel north,
following the river upstream. The first two villages are Lirac and Tavel: they
produce some of the best rosé wines of France. A little further along the Route
des Vins you come to the old, walled village of St Laurent-des Arbres. Next is
the St-Victor-La-Coste; looming high above it is an extraordinary huge
part-ruined, part-occupied, fortification called le Castella. From here the
road continues back northwards past the small wine villages of Laudun and
Chusclan and then for a while along the river bank into Pont-St Esprit.

The alternative route goes west from Villeneuve-lès-Avignon through the
villages of Saze, Domazan, Théziers and then northward via Pouzilhac (on
the N 86), Gaujac and Thesque to the town of Bagnols-sur-Cèze. This is a
beautiful, quiet rural route and like all the Côtes du Rhône circuits, it is very
well signposted. Instead of returning directly to Pont-St Esprit along the
N 86, a really delightful detour can be made by following the route through St

The wine village of Flassan in the foothills of Mont Ventoux to the north east of Carpentras

Gervais, St Michel-d'Euzet and St Laurent de Carnois to la Roque-sur-Cèze, a little village perched on high. Nearby, at the Cascade du Sautadet, the river spills into a series of rocky crevices; flat rocks beside the cascade invite you to sit and dream. A little further along the D 980 is Cornillon, its walls rising up from the sheer cliff on which it is built. Doubling back a little towards Bagnols-sur-Cèze you will find a small road on the left, the D 23, which winds up through the village of St Laurent-de-Carnois and into a wooded valley to the Chartreuse de Valbonne. You can visit the château and buy the wines of the region at a small *caveau* here. Finally, follow the D 23 back into Pont-St Esprit to rejoin the N 86 and the other wine routes.

A Case for Tasting

FROM THE EXOTIC WHITES of the northern Rhône Valley to the fabled, voluptuous red Hermitage in the centre and the popular 'Côtes' wines of the south, this riverside region encompasses every style.

HERMITAGE

This is the greatest red wine of the Rhône, dense in colour, opulently aromatic of the Syrah grape from which it is made, rich and complex in flavour. A wine to buy young when it is affordable (100FF upwards) and keep ten years. The Chave family's vineyards on the Hermitage hill have been passed from father to son since 1481. The wine is superb.

CROZES HERMITAGE

Wines from vineyards peripheral to Hermitage itself are sold under this name. They are less concentrated in flavour and mature earlier, but have a good silky Syrah-grape character. Cave des Clairmonts wines (which include a good, fresh white Crozes) are excellent value at 30 to 40FF.

CHÂTEAUNEUF-DU-PAPE

Wines from this well-known appellation of the southern Rhône are potent – often 13° of alcohol or more – and bursting with the rich flavour of the Grenache grape. Quality does vary from grower to grower, so choose a good one such as Lucien Michel of Le Vieux Donjon, Domaine du Père Caboche, or Chante Cigale.

GIGONDAS

Vineyards clustered around the foot of the great Mont Ventoux east of Orange in the southern Rhône produce this profoundly flavoured and intense red wine. Good to drink in vigorous youth, or to keep for a decade to develop silky maturity. Domaine St Gayan is Gigondas at its very best.

CÔTES DU RHONE

A veritable ocean of wine is made under this generic name – much of it poor value even at under 10FF a bottle. The best wines can be ripe, fruity and elegant, and worth seeking out. Rasteau is a superior 'village' wine from the Domaine St Gayan of Gigondas.

VIN DE PAYS DE L'ARDÈCHE

Honest, slurpable red wine from the vast Ardèche *vin de pays* area can have real vibrance and juiciness of flavour when made from the Syrah grape. Good value at well under 10FF. The co-operative at St Désirat makes exceptional wine at the price.

LIRAC

Neighbouring Châteauneuf-du-Pape, the village of Lirac makes wines which in many ways rival the more famous appellation – except for celebrity and price. The lush, vibrant red and rosé Liracs from Armand Maby richly deserve comparison.

TAVEL

Armand Maby, for many years Mayor of the village of Tavel, has done much to elevate its rosé wines to their exalted status as the best pinks in the world. La Forcadière is beautifully coloured, fresh and delicately flavoured. Maby also makes a crisp, fruity and zesty white Tavel.

CONDRIEU

'Its musky may-blossom fragrance, so redolent of Spring, and delicious lightly spicy flavour are unique and alluring; something that all wine lovers should experience at first hand.' So says the well known Rhône-wine shipper Robin Yapp of wondrous white Condrieu. Even at more than 100FF a bottle, he does have a point!

MUSCAT DE BEAUMES-DE-VENISE

Flourishing under the torrid sun that roasts the vineyards around the village of Beaumes-de-Venise in the southern Rhône, the Muscat grape produces straw-gold, nectareous sweet white wine. Chilled, it makes a fine *aperitif* as well as a companion to pudding.

SAINT-PÉRAY

Sparkling wines are something of a rarity in the Rhône, but the *vin mousseux* of St Péray, just across the River Rhône from Valence, are worth looking for. Jean-Louis Thiers makes fruity dry wine by the 'Champagne method'. It goes very well with food.

CLAIRETTE DE DIE

This sparkling wine – labelled 'Tradition' because it is made by a fermentation method long unique to the village of Die – is semi-sweet and quite delectable. It is a blend of Muscat grapes with the delicately flavoured Clairette variety, and appealingly low in alcohol at 7.5°.

Languedoc

*Above: A Springtime landscape in the Languedoc vineyards near the
wine village of Cabrerolles
Left: Baskets of Grenache grapes awaiting transportation to the presses
near the wine village of St Joseph
Following pages: The gorges of the River Orb between the wine villages
of Vieussan and Roquebrun in Languedoc*

*L*ANGUEDOC ENJOYS THE warm, sunny climate of the Mediterranean in
which the grape vine thrives. This is one of the main wine-producing
regions in France, the origin of millions of bottles of *Vin de Table* and a major
contributor to the wine lake. Its wine is known more for its quantity than for
its quality. However, although few truly great wines are produced in
Languedoc, there are many good and satisfying ones to be tried and the
traveller will find the countryside and villages fascinating to explore. The
Mediterranean coast is always crowded in the summer months, but even a
short distance inland there is a wild and spectacular landscape largely
undiscovered by tourists.

Ironically, in view of its lack of great wines, Languedoc is considered to be
the birthplace of the French wine industry. The vine is probably indigenous to
the area, but its cultivation dates from the Roman occupation in the second
century BC. Then, wine was imported from Italy through the Roman port of
Narbo Martius, now Narbonne; it is this trade which encouraged the
Narbonnais to cultivate the vine and produce their own wine. Winemaking
became so important to the region that legend has it that when the Visigoths
invaded the city of Béziers in the fifth century they met no resistance because
everyone was out in the vineyards harvesting the grapes.

The area's Roman heritage is also evident in a wealth of architectural
remains: there are ruined ramparts, aqueducts, amphitheatres, bridges and
churches throughout the region. The Roman amphitheatre in Nîmes, for
example, is the most perfectly preserved in the world.

*A roadside sign among the vineyards near the wine village of Fos near
Faugères in the Languedoc*

The region's name is derived from its mother tongue, literally the *Langue
d'Oc*, *oc* being the regional word for 'yes'; the northern parts of France, where
'yes' was *oil*, now *oui*, was known as the *Langue d'Oil*.

T H E   W I N E S

There is a considerable variety of wine to be found in the region. As well as
reds, whites and rosés of varying quality and character, there are also a
number of dessert or *Vin Doux Naturel* wines with the *appellation contrôlée*
classification, such as Muscat de Frontignan, Muscat de Lunel and Muscat
de Mireval as well as sparkling wines and brandies. There are several other
appellation contrôlée wines such as Clairette de Bellegarde, Clairette du
Languedoc, Fitou, Minervois, Corbières, La Clape, Picpoul-de-Pinet,
Coteaux de Saint Christol, Saint Saturnin, Montpeyroux, Faugères, and
Saint Chinian.

There are just two VDQS wines, Côtes de la Malepère and Cabardès. The
main volume of the production is *vin de table* and *vin de pays*, and some wine goes
into the manufacture of vermouths and *apéritif* wines such as *Byhrr*. There is a
large number of different grape types used, because of the widely varying
nature of the soil and location of the vineyards; they include the Carignan,
Grenache, Aramon, Cinsault and Maccabéo. The Muscat is used for much of
the dessert wine.

T H E   C U I S I N E

Perhaps the best-known dish of the region is *cassoulet*, named after the covered
dish in which it is cooked, the *cassolle*. It is a very rich combination of meats
such as lamb, duck or goose *confits*, pork or bacon and sausages, baked with
onions, garlic and tomatoes and white beans. Then there are the famous

The medieval village of St Guilhem-le-Desert which shelters in the gorges of the River Herault

Toulouse sausages, *anchoide* (anchovy paste) from Nîmes, game and pâtés, wild mushrooms and wonderful vegetable stews. Fresh and saltwater fish are found in abundance, but the people of Languedoc are still fond of dried salt cod; in *Morue à la minervoise* it is cooked with the red Minervois wine, onions, olive oil, garlic, anchovies and olives. *Pelardon* is a favourite goats'-milk cheese; it is sold in small discs and has a soft texture and delicate nutty flavour.

THE ROUTE DES VINS *Michelin map 83*

The Route des Vins is very extensive, stretching south from Nîmes nearly to Carcassonne. It is best to divide it into four separate tours; of course, you can combine two or more of them to suit your own interests. The route is quite well signposted – the signs are rather small but are sensibly sited. In places the route is quite circuitous and a certain amount of backtracking is necessary, but the countryside is so splendid that this simply increases the pleasure of the journey.

There are other wine communities outside the official wine route that are also worth visiting – for instance, those producing *Vin de Sable* (literally, wine of the sand) in the sandy soil around the medieval, fortified town of Aigues-Mortes on the edge of the Camargue, or Costières du Gard, made just south of Nîmes. Clairette de Bellegarde, a dry white *appellation contrôlée* wine, comes from the same area, while Muscat de Lunel, a dessert wine, is produced nearby.

The first circuit begins just to the west of Nîmes, in the small wine village of Langlade. Here, the vineyards are not intensively cultivated and the broad valley through which the road sweeps is chequered with a patchwork of vineyards, meadows and crops such as asparagus and rapeseed; the hills on either side, although quite steep, are not very high. As you travel

westwards the land becomes more undulating and the distant mountains more dominant. Pass the small walled town of Sommières on the banks of the River Vidourle and continue south on the D 105 through St Christol, Vérargues and St Geniès; the hillsides here are more densely covered with vines. As the Route des Vins turns northwards towards the wine villages of St Drézéry and Fontanès the landscape begins to change, taking on a wilder and more rugged character with steep, rocky outcrops and the dense, wiry *maquis* dotted with pine trees. Soon the large, distant, conical shape of the Pic St Loup appears to the west. The road continues northward to the small villages of Valflaunès, Lauret and Claret, on the D 17, which now winds its way through dense pine forests. This is an ideally tranquil place in which to stretch your legs or have a picnic lunch. Corconne, the most northerly point of this part of the wine route, is a charming small village of old stone houses set at the foot of two cliffs in a ravine.

From here follow the same road back to Valflaunès, where a small road, the D 1e, branches off to wind around the dramatic Pic St Loup. This countryside is full of colour; the steep, rocky hillsides are covered with *maquis*, wild flowers

The lake of Salagou, to the north west of
Clermont-l'Herault, a popular place for water sports and camping

and herbs and shaded by pine trees; it is popular with the local people, who come here to walk, climb and picnic at the weekends. In the nearby village of Nôtre-Dame-de-Londres is a small twelfth-century château.

The Route des Vins now leads to the small villages of St Matthieu-de-Tréviers, Cazevieille and St Jean-de-Cuculles, the latter teetering on a hilltop. The quiet road through this region weaves through steep, rocky hillsides with pine forests and there are frequent beautiful views, with the Pic St Loup constantly dominating the landscape. It's worth visiting the little medieval village of Les Matelles; its ramparts, fortified gateways, narrow, steeply winding streets, archways and tunnels are all in miniature.

The next important wine village, some way to the west, is Montpeyroux, which produces well-respected *appellation contrôlées* reds and rosés, as does the nearby village of St Saturnin. An essential minor detour here is to the Gorges de l'Hérault and the village of St Guilhem-le-Désert. Although these gorges are not as deep and extensive as those of say Verdun or the Tarn, nonetheless

*The Château de Grezan, once a Templar fortress, is now a
well-respected producer of Languedoc wines*

they are very impressive. You can climb down to the riverside quite easily in
many places and enjoy the solitude surrounded by the majestic rocks. The
village of St Guilhem is built along a deep cleft in the side of the gorges, its
tiny, narrow, stone houses with their brown-tiled roofs nestling under a
massive rock looming high above. The Grotte de Clamouse is close by; you
should linger here for a while.

Another worthwhile detour in this region is to the lake of Salagou, where
you can windsurf, sail and canoe; there are also camping facilities. Nearby is
the Cirque de Mourèze, a place with strange dolomitic pinnacles with a tiny
village in the middle. This is the most westerly point of the first circuit and the
route now begins to head back towards Montpellier through the wine villages
of Aspiran, Lézignan-la-Cèbe, Montbazin, Pignan and Lavérune, the latter
virtually a suburb of the city. The lovely Abbaye de Valmagne, one of the
most beautiful buildings in Languedoc, is situated between the villages of
Montagnac and Villeveyrac. Montpellier has been an important wine centre
for many centuries and was also a leading producer of liqueurs. Today its
importance is just as great as it houses the Ecole Nationale Supérieure
Agronomique, the Ecole d'Oenologie (College of Wine) and the Ecole de
Viticulture, and as such is the main centre in France for the study of the
cultivation of the vine.

The second circuit of the Côtes du Languedoc Routes des Vins starts just
north of the town of Agde in the small wine village of Pinet, which produces a
wine called Picpoul-de-Pinet. The Picpoul is a grape used to produce the
rather thin wine from which Cognac is distilled, but here the soil and climate
combine favourably to produce a well-thought-of dry white wine. The wine
road continues northward on the D 161 towards the town of Pézenas, an
attractive old town with narrow streets and some distinguished buildings,

where Molière spent several winters. In nearby Caux there is a twelfth-century church and the remains of ramparts from the sixth century. From Pézenas the Route des Vins continues along the D 13 through the wine villages of Roujan and Gabian towards Faugères; there are extensive vineyards along this road, and many opportunities to stop and taste the wine. Just north of Roujan; set among the vineyards, is the charming château of Cassan. As in the rest of the Languedoc, most of the wine here is made by small producers who own only a few hectares. Consequently the *Cave Co-opérative* plays an important economic role; sometimes these vast establishments almost dwarf the tiny villages that give them their name. A few kilometres off the main wine route, along tiny country lanes, there are many small wine-producing villages, such as Fos and Roquessels, which is perched on a pinnacle of rock. If you take these small detours you will discover some tranquil countryside – a beautiful stretch of road with splendid views is the D 15 from Neffiès to Cabrières, while the *caveau* in Nizas, north of Pézenas, is in an attractive château in the centre of the village.

Faugères, a very small and quiet village, is an important wine centre for the surrounding producers and makes excellent red and rosé wines. The nearby small town of Laurens has steep, narrow streets surmounted by an imposing château. The Château de Grezan, close by, is well worth a visit; the restored building was once a Templars fortress and it stands in the middle of extensive

Early Spring in the Languedoc vineyard near Langlade to the south west of Nîmes

vineyards with a backdrop of distant mountains; you can taste and buy the château's excellent red wine here. The owner showed me the *caves* in which about two dozen vast casks about 5 metres in diameter were lined up along each wall. They are over 150 years old, he told me, and the oak staves are held together by 3 tonnes of metal; each holds 25,000 litres of wine. The nearby town of Autignac has a wine co-operative and a co-operative distillery for the making of *eau de vie*.

Towards the villages of Caussiniojouis and Cabrerolles the distant mountains of the Haut Languedoc begin to loom larger and the countryside becomes hillier and more rugged. The region has magnificent scenery and

An old house in the curious small village of Barrubio in the Minervois
wine region
Following pages: Vineyards in the valley of the River Cesse with the
medieval village of Minerve in the background

there are unexpected vistas at every twist and turn of the narrow, winding road. It is very quiet – you can drive for an hour or more without meeting another car or even seeing a house – and there is virtually no sign of habitation except for the well-tended vineyards which pattern the hillsides.

From St Nazaire-de-Ladarex to Roquebrun the wine road follows the course of the River Orb. The small village of Roquebrun, at the head of the

A roadside sign near the wine town of St Chinian in the Languedoc vineyards

valley nestling below the mountain, spreads up the hillside to a ruined tower. Follow the wine route to Vieussan, another dramatically sited village – this time above a steep cliff beside the river where the hillsides are so steep that the vineyards are terraced, with dry stone walls to hold the soil. Both these villages have a microclimate in which oranges and mimosa as well as the vines flourish and the landscape becomes almost alpine in character. The road continues now along the D 177 towards the village of Berlou. As you wind up out of the valley to the top of the mountain there are a series of quite spectacular panoramas. After St Chinian, which is an important wine centre, the Route des Vins continues along the main road, the N 112, to Cébazan and south to Quarante, the last village on this leg of the wine route.

The wine-growing region of the Minervois is adjacent to St Chinian and has its own small, signposted circuit. The most convenient place to start the Minervois circuit is in the small village of Montouliers, near Quarante, the last village on the previous tour. Head towards St Jean-de-Minervois through landscape that is quite different from that covered in the previous tour. Nearby are the curious, tiny wine villages of Gimios and Barroubio with houses built of large, rough, white stones; the vineyards in this region are also covered with white, flinty stones, which at times create the illusion of a snowfall. From here, the wine road continues through the villages of Agel and la Caunette towards Minèrve. The Romanesque church at Minèrve contains an altar dated 456, supposed to be the oldest altar in France. There is an archaeological museum here and the remains of medieval fortifications. The route continues through the villages of Azillanet, Cesseras and Siran towards Caunes-Minervois. The vineyards here, in what is now a much flatter landscape, are very extensive and opportunities to stop and taste wine are frequent. The grottoes of Limousis are close by; they can be visited with a

*A quiet country road which leads through the vineyards to the south east
of Nîmes*

guide on Sundays and holidays only in the afternoons. The Minervois Route
des Vins completes its circuit via the wine villages of Laure, Rieux-Minervois
(where there is an interesting octagonal church), Azille, Olonzac, Pouzols
and Argeliers back to Montouliers.

The final part of the Languedoc Route des Vins is concentrated in the
Montagne de la Clape, a region very near the sea, between Narbonne and
Narbonne-Plage. The circuit winds through the small villages of Salles-
d'Aude, Fleury, Gruissan, Armissan and Vinassan. The Massif de la Clape is
a strange hump of a hill set on the flat coastal plain from which it rises quite
dramatically. It is a quite curious landscape; on top it is rocky, rugged and
even a little bleak, covered with *maquis* and dotted with pine trees. It has a
rather remote and not-of-this-world atmosphere. There are some impressive
views from the small road that leads to the village of Armissan displaying the
unusual nature of the landscape of la Clape. The wines here have an excellent
reputation, particularly the white *appellation contrôlée* wine with its dry but
fruity character well suited to the seafood which is available in abundance in
the region. The route is by the sea around Gruissan, an old circular fortified
town which in fact stands on a lagoon, and there are lovely pine forests
between the water and the mountain. Close by is the Château de Bouis, one of
many places where you can taste and buy the local wines. From here it is a
short distance to the Autoroute A 9 which will take you back northwards or
on to Perpignan.

A Case for Tasting

THE REPUTATION OF LANGUEDOC WINES, particularly the hefty, delicious reds, has soared in recent years. But the wines remain excellent value – especially from this selection of top estates.

FITOU

The warming red wines of this famous appellation draw their intense colour and deep concentration of flavour from the judicious blending of Grenache and Carignan grapes – with fine tuning from half a dozen other varieties. Best to drink around five years old. The Producteurs du Mont Tauch make outstanding wines.

FAUGÈRES

Red wines from this appellation are often described as 'rustic' – darkly coloured and full of concentrated, spicy flavour. Château Grezan's Cuvée Arnaud Lubac is exceptional: aged in oak casks, smooth and opulent, to be kept up to a decade before drinking. At about 30FF, very good value indeed.

VIN DE PAYS DE L'AUDE

Most of the huge quantity of *vin de pays* produced in the Aude is red, and some of it very good. This white wine from the now-ubiquitous Chardonnay grape is fresh, appley and zingy – a delicious example of the developing talent among Mediterranean winemakers. Definitely a wine to drink young.

BLANQUETTE DE LIMOUX

This is the wonderfully fresh and lively sparkling wine from just north-east of Languedoc, made from Mauzac, Chardonnay and Chenin Blanc grapes. Pierre Robert, a winemaker at Pieusse, produces an exceptionally flavoursome *brut* (very dry) example. The name Blanquette comes from the downy fluff that coats the leaves of the Mauzac vine.

MUSCAT DE FRONTIGNAN

One of several appellations making *vin doux naturel* and *vin de liqueur* from the super-sweet Muscat grape. These are extremely sweet, raisiny dessert wines made by adding spirit to the grape juice before it ferments. Stick to the lighter *vin doux* – they are delicious.

MAS DE DAUMAS GASSAC

This wine is ranked a mere *vin de pays de l'Hérault* but by rights should have an *appellation contrôlée* designation to itself. It is the greatest wine of Languedoc, and one of the best made anywhere in France. Beautiful Bordeaux-style red from the Cabernet Sauvignon grape, for keeping at least ten years.

SAINT-CHINIAN

Wines from this appellation have a name for being lighter in colour and body than other Languedoc reds. Domaine des Jougla's harmonious 'Tradition' wine, matured in oak casks, is an example with real class – so don't be put off by the distracting label. Good value at under 30FF.

COSTIÈRES DU GARD

Adjoining the Rhône River at Languedoc's eastern limits, this new appellation makes many fine reds with light body and softly fruity flavours. Domaine St Louis la Perdrix's splendid Cuvée Marianne, 'selected amongst the best vintages for its bouquet, rich colour, subtlety, fullness and fruitiness,' is a bargain at around 20FF.

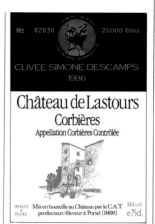

CORBIÈRES

Another name now achieving worldwide recognition, Corbières is a vast appellation of more than 50,000 acres. The reds can be deliciously smooth and spicy in flavour – and high in alcohol. This very fine oak-aged Corbières from Château de Lastours is 14°. Drink within five years.

PICPOUL DE PINET

Pinet is one of ten villages in the large Côteaux du Languedoc appellation entitled to name themselves on labels. Picpoul is a grape variety producing a zesty and likeable dry white wine to drink thoroughly chilled within a few months of the vintage. Gaujal's wine costs 20FF.

MINERVOIS

'It has a powerful bouquet, with the very complex yet harmonious scent and taste of thyme, cinnamon and spices,' says Jean Maris of his red Minervois – a wine of considerably more finesse than most of the rather coarse products of this appellation. The wines taste better after a year or two, but should be drunk within five. Under 20FF.

LA CLAPE

La Clape is another of the Côteaux du Languedoc villages. The red wines can be rather lean – though characterful. The whites are more reliable, being well coloured and full of assertive fruity flavour. Excellent with Mediterranean seafood.

Provence

*Above: Vineyards in early Spring near the wine village of Carces to the
north east of Brignoles*
*Left: Typical Provençal houses in the old hill-top town of Bargemon to the
north east of Draguignan*
*Following pages: A flock of sheep grazing below the old trees to the
north east of La Motte*

ℰ NDLESS BLUE SKIES, olive groves, wild thyme and lavender fields, garlic,
pine trees, parched rust-coloured soil, sea, sea, sea . . . this is
Provence. It is hardly surprising that the south of France has been one of the
most popular European tourist destinations for generations. Provence has
one of the most beautiful stretches of coastline in the whole of the
Mediterranean. It also has majestic mountains, wild gorges and cascading
rivers, as well as vast forests and green, fertile valleys. Its cultural heritage is
fascinating and there is a wealth of small, unspoilt villages, many in
spectacular settings. Added to all this is the perennial attraction of the
powerful Mediterranean sun and the warm and benevolent climate it creates.

Provence also possesses extensive vineyards which produce a range of good
wines. The other, more obvious, attractions of the region are so appealing,
however, that many visitors remain virtually unaware of what the vineyards
offer. The principal wine-growing area of Provence is in the region of the Var,
bordered by Toulon in the west and Fréjus in the east and extending as far
north as Draguignan. Within this area the wine route offers the traveller every
aspect of the Provençal countryside, from breathtakingly beautiful coastal
scenery to wild and rugged mountainscapes and peaceful, pastoral valleys.

THE WINES

The predominant wines of Provence, Côtes de Provence, have an *appellation
controlée* classification. Although red, white and rosé are all made, the region is

best known for its rosés and indeed some are among the best made in France; they are very dry with a high alcohol content, a good body and a fruity aroma. VDQS rosés (and some undistinguished reds and whites) come from vineyards of Coteaux de Pierrevert. There are a number of other *appellation contrôlée* wines such as Coteaux d'Aix-en-Provence, Cassis, Bandol, Bellet and Palette, and some *vin de pays* including Les Maures Coteaux Varois, Mont Caume and Argens.

Cinsault, Grenache, Carignane, Tibouren and Peccoui Touar grapes are used to make the rosés and reds; and the white wines are made from the Picpoul, Clairette, Sémillon and Ugni Blanc grapes.

THE CUISINE

Grapes are not the only important crop in Provence: the olive tree is almost as plentiful (there is a Route de l'huile d'olive) and olive oil is essential to the region's cuisine. *Aïoli*, a garlic-flavoured mayonnaise made with olive oil, is served with seafood or raw vegetables. There are wonderful vegetable stews such as *ratatouille* of aubergines and peppers cooked in olive oil. *Salade niçoise* is a combination of tomatoes, olives, capers, potatoes, beans, lettuce, anchovies and tuna. *Pan bagna* is a *baguette* filled with anchovies, tomato and capers. The rich, tangy sauce called *tapenade* is made with olives, capers, tuna and anchovies; it is delicious with hard-boiled eggs. *Sauce provençale* is served with fish, meat and vegetable dishes; tomatoes, garlic and shallots are gently simmered in white wine and olive oil, and seasoned with parsley and basil. *Pissaladière* is a flat bread dough covered with olives, anchovies, onions and tomatoes, which is similar to the Italian pizza.

An evening landscape in the vineyard-covered countryside near Le Plan-de-la-Tour in the Massifs des Maures

An old farmhouse surrounded by vineyards between Carces and Montfort-sur-Argens

With all of these regional specialities you should drink a chilled Côtes de Provence rosé. Another speciality of the region, traditionally served at Easter and Christmas, is Vin Cuit (cooked wine), made by boiling newly pressed, unfermented grape juice until it is reduced to about a third of its volume and adding a measure of *marc* or *eau de vie*.

THE ROUTE DES VINS *Michelin map 84*

The Route des Vins is quite extensive and it would take several weeks to explore it properly. Although the distances may not appear great on the map, most of the roads are very narrow and winding, with numerous hairpin bends, and it can often take an hour or two to cover only 10 kilometres – especially when there are so many temptations to stop and admire the views or to explore tiny villages. The route is well signposted and is essentially a circular tour, but it incorporates a number of detours. If you are staying on the coast, you could begin the tour at either St Tropez or Hyères; if travelling on the Autoroute A 8 (*La Provençale*) start at Brignoles or Fréjus.

Officially the Route des Vins begins in Toulon, a busy port and the main French naval base (established by Louis XIV). It leads to Hyères, a resort town that was fashionable as long ago as the eighteenth century; there are a number of important *domaines* with *caves* here where you can sample the wines, and just off the coast are the beautiful islands of Porquerolles, Levant and Port-Cros. The wine road leaves the coast at this point and crosses the wide, fertile valley of the River Réal Martin to Pierrefeu-du-Var. The landscape is quite flat and the vineyards are extensive here, and you can see the mountains in the distance. It is particularly handsome in springtime when the new shoots of the vines and the trees in blossom contrast vividly with the rich,

Vineyards near the wine village of Carces photographed in early Spring

red-brown soil. From Pierrefeu the road leads to Cuers, which has a number of interesting old buildings, including a sixteenth-century church, as well as a *Cave Co-opérative* and some private *caves*. The wine road continues along the main road, the N 97, through the wine villages of Puget-Ville with its thirteenth-century Saracen tower, Carnoules and Pignans, from which you can make a small detour to the viewpoint of Nôtre Dame des Anges. The next village is Gonfaron, where, legend has it, a donkey once flew, and then you come to le Luc, a colourful town on the busy N 7. It is an important wine centre, and there are nine *caves* that you can visit. Also of interest are the twelfth-century clocktower and a Romanesque chapel.

The wine route now doubles back along the N 7 to the wine village of Flassans-sur-Issole, built around the ruins of an old village and dominated by a privately owned feudal castle. Here the wine road heads north again on the D 13 to Cabasse and Carcès, an old olive oil-milling town. From here a detour can be made to the famous twelfth-century Abbaye de Thoronet, a superb example of Romanesque architecture, built by the Cistercians and restored by order of Prosper Mérimée, the nineteenth-century novelist who was also Inspector-General of Historic Monuments. Just before Carcès the road circumnavigates the Lac de Carcès, an artificial lake that supplies water to many of the coastal resorts. This is excellent countryside for picnicking. Nearby are the jagged red cliffs and quarries of the bauxite mines, which lend a rather surrealist air to the landscape.

The route continues west to Montfort-sur-Argens, almost as noteworthy for being the home of Louis-Joseph Lambart, the man who invented reinforced concrete, as for its Templar castle and twelfth-century church. You can take a detour here to the tiny village of Correns, set in a peaceful vine-clad valley beside the little Argens river. The main route continues north to Cotignac, set at the foot of a high, sheer cliff under a ruined watchtower. Sit in an outdoor café shaded by enormous plane trees on Cotignac's broad main street and really absorb the Provençal atmosphere. There are caves cut into the cliffs, an eleventh-century priory church and the remains of an oil mill, and the Chapel of Nôtre-Dame de Grâce, a famous sanctuary since the time of Louis XIII, set on a hill opposite the village; it can be reached by a small road near the bridge.

From Cotignac the Route des Vins follows the D 50. The narrow country roads are lined with dry-stone walls, which are also used to terrace the vineyards and olive groves. When the wild flowers and herbs are in full bloom and the air is heady with their fragrance, everything seems absolutely perfect. You get to the hilltown of Entrecasteaux next. It is dominated by an eleventh-century château, which is privately owned but allows visitors and offers Chambre d'hôte accommodation, it has two old churches and a chapel built above it. As you drive towards St Antonin du Var, look back at the village – it is very dramatic against the steep wooded hillsides.

The route continues towards Draguignan via the village of Lorgues, where there are many interesting old buildings including a Saracen gate, ancient ramparts and towers and an old oil mill now used as an art gallery. You can make several detours from here. Go to Flayosc to see a typical village of the region; its village square is shaded by plane trees and there is an ancient

Rooftops in the old quarter of Draguignan

Old mellowed houses overlook the shady square in the village of Lorgues
to the south west of Draguignan

fountain, which is quintessentially Provençal. Visit Villecroze (to the north-west along the D 10), a high mountain village, for its wine and for the spectacular views over the surrounding landscape. And walk up the narrow winding streets of nearby Tourtour, which is at an altitude of 1630 metres, and enjoy the views; it also has a private château and a few old towers.

The shady streets and squares of old Draguignan contain some fine buildings, including an Ursuline convent that houses the town's museum and

library, a Roman gate and a sixteenth-century clock-tower. From here a detour can be made through the enchanting medieval hill villages of Callas, Bargemon, Seillans, Fayence and Callian; each twist and turn of the road which connects them reveals a new and breathtaking vista. Callian and Seillans are very small and delightful; the latter has a Saracen gate and an eleventh-century feudal castle perched high up above its tiny houses. Continue south on the D 4 through the villages of St Paul-en-Forêt and Bagnols-en-Forêt, which, as their names suggest, are set deep in the cork forest that borders the mountains of the Esterel. There are many good picnic

spots on the first part of the drive through forested hillsides then, as it winds round the sides of the mountains, the road becomes more austere and mountainous with panoramic views of the valleys below. At Bagnols-en-Forêt you rejoin the main wine route to Trans-en-Provence and la Motte along the D 47. This too is a ruggedly beautiful road through forests and mountains. At one point, where the road runs alongside a rugged, red gorge, just a short distance from the road, you can see a dramatic outcrop of rock and impressive views down into the gorge.

From Bagnols-en-Forêt the road winds down towards the coast and the town of Fréjus, the oldest Roman city in Gaul. Julius Caesar founded it, Augustus built up its harbour and Agricola was born here. There are many important Roman remains, including an amphitheatre where bullfights are held in summer, part of an aqueduct and ramparts. Fréjus was destroyed in the tenth century, but got a new lease of life 500 years later when its fine cathedral was built.

The wine road continues west along the N 7 through the wine villages of Puget-sur-Argens and le Muy to les Arcs, an important wine centre. Take a short detour to Roquebrune-sur-Argens where the biggest mulberry tree in

*A street scene in the old town of Bargemon in the mountains to the north
east of Draguignan*

The eleventh-century feudal castle of Seillans, a hill village to the north east of Draguignan

the South of France grows. The village is situated beneath a red rock which rises from the flat coastal plain, and you can drive around it through the surrounding vineyards, or walk through its wooded slopes to a small chapel nestling in a cleft half-way up. From les Arcs the route continues through the small wine village of Taradeau to Vidauban, with its seventeenth-century château. The Routes des Vins continues on the D 48 through the Massif des Maures; there are dramatic views at every turn as the road winds steeply through forested hillsides. The ancient hilltop villages of la Garde-Freinet and Grimaud are a delight. particularly Grimaud, a medieval walled town with a Renaissance chapel and a ruined eleventh-century castle. A short detour to the west from la Garde-Freinet takes you to the Roches Blanches, where there are superb views over the village and surrounding countryside. A second detour can be made, this time to the east, over the Col de Vignon to the village of Plan-de-la-Tour.

The sophisticated and crowded St Tropez is the next town on the wine route. Early this century, long before Brigitte Bardot, it was a favourite summer resort of the Neo-Impressionist painters, including Bonnard and Matisse. You should visit the Co-opérative du Golfe de St Tropez, and the important *domaine* of Château de Minuty, which is nearby. Every May, St Tropez honours its patron saint in a street procession that is quite unique to this part of France – a wonderful spectacle. From here a small scenic road winds up into the mountains above the town through Gassin, where the views over the gulf are awe-inspiring. The road continues to the hilltown of Ramatuelle, a lovely medieval village where a large, ancient elm tree grows in

Above: Early Spring in the Côtes de Provence vineyards in the valley of
the River Argens near les Arcs
Right: The rooftops of Bormes les Mimosas, an attractive coastal town
on the picturesque Corniche des Maures

the square. Follow the route over the Col de Collebasse to la Croix-Valmer, with spectacular views down to the sea.

There are two options now: you can continue along the coast through the resorts of Cavalaire-sur-Mer and Rayol to le Lavandou and Bormes-les-Mimosas, or you can return inland and follow the N 98 to Cogolin and la Môle. On the coastal route, the road follows the beautiful coastline. The walled town of Bormes-les-Mimosas is particularly pretty, built on the side of a steeply sloping hillside a few kilometres from the sea. This stretch of road will be very crowded and congested in the summer months, though, and perhaps should be avoided then.

The alternative route runs along the valley of the river Môle, whose banks are lined with tall reeds. These are cut and dried and made into clarinet reeds and pipes in Cogolin, which is also known for its carpets and silk yarn. From la Môle you can take a winding scenic road over the Col du Canadel to the sea; at the top there is a sudden, almost startling view of the sea far down below. The Route des Vins completes its circuit after passing through la Londe-les-Maures, on the N 98.

In addition to the main wine circuit there is a small tour further west towards Aix-en-Provence, through the small wine villages of Puyloubier, Pourrières, Pourcieux, Trets, Peynier and Rousset, in the foothills of the Montagne Sainte Victoire. The small wine-growing communities in the coastal resorts of Bandol and Cassis, between Toulon and Marseille, and in the region of Bellet in the Var valley near Nice, are also worth visiting both for their interesting wines and for their delightful locations.

A Case for Tasting

THE VINEYARDS OF THE FRENCH RIVIERA and its mountainous hinterland provide some delightful surprises for wine lovers – and a pleasing diversion from the brash attractions of the coastal resorts.

L'ESTANDON ROSÉ

Coral pink, mildly aromatic and quaffably refreshing, this is a firm favourite with appreciative French holidaymakers in the bars all along the Côte d'Azur. It is made at Cuers just behind Toulon, and along with its red and white stablemates ranks as a Côtes de Provence *appellation contrôlée*.

CLOS STE MAGDELEINE

Cassis is a highly picturesque – if seasonally overpopulated – fishing village east of Marseilles with its own small stretch of vineyards immediately behind. Clos Ste Magdeleine, among the encroaching luxury villa developments, makes lovely scented dry white wine – perfect to drink with the local fish.

CHÂTEAU DE CRÉMAT

The Bellet appellation lies in the hills behind the urban sprawl of Nice. Crémat's vines include several species unique to this district, and the wines are accordingly distinctive. The white is zesty and fresh, but intensely flavoured, the rosé delightful – and the red sweet and cherry-like.

DOMAINE DE TRÉVALLON

The Côteaux des Baux vineyards at St Rémy midway between Arles and Avignon are not renowned for their wines – with one notable exception. Trévallon makes magnificent red wine from a 60/40 ratio of Cabernet Sauvignon and Syrah grapes in a vineyard that appears to be of pure broken bauxite rock. For drinking at 5 to 15 years old.

DOMAINE RICHEAUME

This estate east of Aix-en-Provence is run on an organic-culture basis, and makes exciting wines. The red is soft and full flavoured, and will improve with keeping for a few years. Other reds include 'varietals' – each made with just one grape variety – of very high quality.

CHÂTEAU LA CANORGUE

Côtes du Lubéron is the appellation immediately north of the Côteaux d'Aix, and for years had a name for making dismal wine. Not so now, for winemakers such as Jean-Pierre Margan of La Canorgue are making intensely fruity reds and clean, excitingly fresh whites of the highest standard.

MAS DE LA ROUVIÈRE

This is one of the famous wines of Bandol – the *chic* coastal resort now becoming equally fashionable for its vineyards. Mas (the word means farmhouse) white wine is supple, fruity and dry, and there is an equally good rosé. The red is rich, dark and thoroughly un-Provençale in character; very fine wine best kept a few years.

VIN DE PAYS DU MONT CAUME

This good-quality wine is granted only the status of a *vin de pays* because it is made with the Cabernet Sauvignon grape – not a variety permitted under the local *appellation contrôlée* rules. It is a smooth, blackcurranty red full of fruitiness – made in the hills behind Bandol.

DOMAINE DES HAUTS ST JEAN

This is a pleasingly fresh dry white made 50 per cent with the famous Sauvignon grape (not, in fact, a variety that is supposed to be used under local *appellation contrôlée* rules) and 50 per cent Rolle variety. Henri-Richard Pawlowski is one of many new winemakers to set up in Provence since the 1970s.

CHÂTEAU DE LA GAUDE

High up in the hills behind Aix-en-Provence, this vineyard arranged around a rather grand *château* produces excellent, good-value (around 20FF) red and rosé wines under the Côteaux d'Aix *appellation contrôlée*. The dark, juicy red wine is made up with one-fifth Cabernet Sauvignon, the great Bordeaux grape.

CHÂTEAU SIMONE

Just south of Aix, Palette is a tiny appellation of under 50 acres where Simone is one of just two estates. The vines here average 70 years of age – some date back a century – and the resulting red wine is intricately flavoured, rich and harmonious. Best from at least three years after the vintage date.

CHÂTEAU LA ROUVIÈRE

Serious red wine made entirely from the Mourvèdre grape, giving it very long life. Sinewy and tannic while young (under ten years), this is wine to lay down to age, as with claret – but at a relatively modest 40FF a bottle. It is heady, intensely dark in colour, and quite delicious even in its youth.

Wine Buying Guide

A wine-maker's roadside sign in the village of Carces where you can taste and buy the local wines

Viticulturally the Rhône can be split into three regions; the northern Rhône, the middle Rhône, and the southern Rhône. Recently, Rhône wines have been gaining the recognition they undoubtedly deserve, with worldwide interest following the excellent 1983 and 1985 vintages. This means that the prices for the best wines are now beginning to rise to realistic levels, but for the moment they are still good value.

THE NORTHERN RHONE

APPELLATIONS CONTRÔLÉES

Côte Rôtie Here steep slopes grow the Syrah grape that makes a rich yet elegant, perfumed red wine. The region is divided by two distinct soil types into the Côte Brune and the Côte Blonde. Normally the two wines are blended and sold as Côte Rotie, but they also exist individually. Look out too for Guigal's La Mouline and La Landonne. Both are stunning – in quality and also in price.

Under this appellation the red Syrah's richness is granted extra elegance and perfume by the admixture of up to 15 per cent of the aromatic Viognier grape.

Maison Delas, now owned by large vineyard holders and shippers Champagne Deutz and Gelderman, have a cellar for visitors next to their establishment in Tournon, where all the northern Rhône wines can be purchased.

Hermitage A tiny amount of white wine is produced from the Marsanne and Rousanne grapes, but the red wine from Syrah is king here. The granite mountain gives a richness and sturdiness to the wine that is virtually unequalled in the rest of France. The best comes from the tiny *climat La Chapelle*, perched on top of the mountain and owned by Paul Jaboulet Ainé.

Crozes-Hermitage Both red and white wines are made on more fertile ground around the bottom of the Hermitage mountain. Less rich and complex than Hermitage, but nevertheless good value.

Cornas This appellation is for red wine only, from the Syrah, making the deepest and richest coloured red wine in France. Needs at least five years' ageing to smooth out the tannin and develop its blackcurranty fruit. The production is small but extremely good value.

St Joseph A more general appellation covering much of the west bank of the northern Rhône. The red wines are more common than the white, but the white is more elegant than the rustic red.

Condrieu A most elegant, expensive and extremely good quality white wine from the low-yielding, aromatic Viognier grape. Very little of the permitted area is cultivated with vines because of the steepness of the slopes, so this wine is fairly rare. It has a

haunting bouquet of apricots and wild flowers and ought not to be missed.

With Condrieu is the smallest appellation in France, Château Grillet. Here the Viognier is cask-aged, giving greater complexity but losing the smell of wild flowers. However, as the production is only 3-4,000 bottles per year, it is extremely expensive and unlikely to be seen outside the district.

St Péray A dry white only, from near Valence. Most is drunk locally, but its full-bodied, lively style makes it worth finding. A *mousseux* is also made here.

THE MIDDLE RHONE

APPELLATIONS CONTRÔLÉES
Clairette-de-Die Dry to sweet sparkling wine is produced here. The dry wine (brut) is made by the *méthode champenoise*, principally from the Clairette grape. The sweeter style (Tradition) is made by the *méthode dioise* or *méthode rurale* with at least 50 per cent Muscat grapes. The sweeter Tradition preserves the grapiness of the Muscat.

A still white wine is also made from the Clairette alone.

Châtillon-en-Diois Red and rosé wines made from a mixture of Burgundian and Rhône red grapes, as well as white wines from the Chardonnay and Aligoté grapes of Burgundy. All are fairly ordinary.

Coteaux du Tricastin An up-and-coming appellation, growing in both size and reputation. The

classic Rhône varieties of grape are planted, making a full, rich, fruity red wine, a small amount of rosé and a still smaller amount of white.

VDQS
Côtes du Vivarais Red, dry white and rosé wine of which the reds are the best and the whites the rarest.

Haut-Comtat Red and rosé only, not seen much nowadays.

THE SOUTHERN RHONE

APPELLATIONS CONTRÔLÉES
Châteauneuf-du-Pape This appellation is famous for its red wine, but white accounts for about 2 per cent of its production. There are 13 legal grape varieties (four of which are white) that can be used to make the red wine, but Grenache, Syrah and Mourvèdre are the most important.

There are two different schools of thought on the making of red wine. The traditionalists in specialized *domaines* made a big, rich, meaty, tannic wine that requires laying down for a main minimum of five years and usually more. The modern trend is to use more Grenache in the *encépagement* to make a less coloured, less tannic, lighter wine that is ready to drink in about three to four years.

The wines produced by the Reflets growers' club are worth looking at, and there are both new and old styles. (The Reflets are a group of about 20 *domaines* who apply more stringent rules to the making of their wine and have the papal cross-keys symbol on their bottles.)

Gigondas Red and rosé wines are produced here, and the rich yet fruity reds are the most interesting. The better wines resemble nearby Châteauneuf-du-Pape.

Vacqueyras Good value, rich red wines. Some can take lengthy ageing along with the better wines of Châteauneuf-du-Pape and Gigondas.

Lirac Red, dry white and rosé wines are all made in this appellation, but the red and the rosé are superior. These wines are well worth finding.

Tavel Dry rosé only. Made principally from the Grenache grape with some Cinsault, the styles vary from oak-aged orangey rosés to the younger, fresher, pink ones.

INDIVIDUAL RHÔNE VILLAGE APPELLATIONS
Beaumes de Venise Good red wines, and a more famous *vin doux naturel* made from the Muscat grape.

Cairanne Rich, deeply coloured, spicy red wines with a small amount of rosé and white.

Chusclan Used to be famous for its rosé but now produces mainly red wine.

Laudun Excellent white wines as well as rosé and red.

Rasteau Some rosé and white wine but the good full-bodied red is more common. However,

Languedoc vineyards near Montpeyroux to the north east of Clermont-l'Herault

this appellation is perhaps better known for the red *vin doux naturel* made from the Grenache grape.

Roaix Mostly red wines.

Rochegude Plummy, deep-coloured red wines only.

Rousset A tiny production, quite rare.

Sablet Mostly red wines.

Saint-Gervais Elegant red wines, but none are great.

Séguret Robust red wines.

Saint-Maurice-sur-Eygues Mostly red wines.

Saint-Pantaléon-les-Vignes Fruity red wines to drink young.

Valréas Dark, velvety red wines.

Vinsobres Full-bodied red wines.

Visan Full, rich, alcoholic red wines and some white.

GENERAL APPELLATIONS
Côtes du Ventoux Making red, dry white and rosé wines of increasingly good quality.

Côtes du Rhône-Villages Red, dry, white and rosé wines from 17

specific communes, making better wine than straight Côtes du Rhône. A good value appellation.

Côtes du Rhône This appellation applies to the whole of the Rhône Valley, but not much wine is made in the north where the steepness of the slopes precludes

Principauté d'Orange Red and rosé only.

LANGUEDOC

This is a region where the wines range from the ordinary to good honest wines. None, however, are great, although research into modern production techniques is elevating the general quality.

APPELLATIONS CONTRÔLÉES
See also *Vins Doux Naturels*

Minervois Well-known red wines and some rosé produced here. This was deservedly promoted from a VDQS to an *appellation contrôlée* in 1985. The reds are deep, rich and quite robust. Although the majority of the production is done by *Caves Co-opératives*, there are some growers who make a better, more complex wine using oak *foudres*. These wines can take four or five years' bottle ageing.

Fitou The first *appellation contrôlée* region in Languedoc (from 1948), producing robust reds from the Carignan and Grenache grapes with small quantities of Cinsault, Mourvèdre, Syrah, Terret Noir and Maccabéo. Best for drinking when about five years old, or even very much older.

Faugères A tiny production of dry white wine from the Clairette grape, but the hearty, rich red from Carignan, Cinsault and Grenache varieties is best known.

Clairette de Languedoc Dry and semi-sweet white wine only, much higher in alcohol than the Clairette-de-Die wines.

St Chinian The largest appellation in Languedoc, producing only fairly inexpensive red wine.

Clairette de Bellegarde A dry white wine from the Clairette grape to drink young.

Costières du Gard Quite a big production, mostly from co-operatives, of red, dry white and rosé wines.

Cabrières Rosé only and the best in Languedoc.

Coteaux de la Méjanelle, Coteaux de St-Christol, Saint-Drézery, St Georges d'Orques Red wines only.

Coteaux de Vérargues, Coteaux du Languedoc, Montpeyroux, Saint-Saturnin Red and rosé wines only.

La Clape, Pic-Saint-Loup, Quatourze Red, dry white and rosé wines.

Picpoul de Pinet A fragrant, fruity, dry white wine from coastal vineyards that grow Picpoul, Clairette and Terret Blanc.

VIN DE PAYS
Vin de Pays du Gard Red, dry white and rosé wines made from Rhône grape varieties but now also with the Bordeaux varieties of Cabernet Sauvignon and Merlot. These wines are generally well made and good value at the more modest end of the scale.

Coteaux Cévenols, Coteaux de Cèze, Coteaux du Pont-du-Gard, Coteaux du Vidourle, Coteaux Flaviens, Côtes du Salavès, Mont Bouquet, Serre de Coiran, Uzège, Vaunage, Vistrenque All produce red, dry white and rosé in the *département* of Gard.

Vin de Pays des Sables du Golfe du Lyon A large area of vineyard, planted on sandbanks and dunes recovered from the sea in the Golfe du Lyon, and stretching across the *départements* of Gard, Hérault and Bouches-du-Rhône. Here a government-backed SICA (similar to a co-operative), known by its brand-

inexpensive, commercial production. The quality can vary immensely within this appellation but most is good quaffing wine.

VDQS
Côtes du Lubéron Red, dry white and rosé wines made east of Avignon in very similar styles to Côtes du Rhône.

VIN DE PAYS
Vin de Pays de l'Ardèche One of the better *Vin de Pays* and improving all the time. Red, dry white and rosé wine. (Also *Vin de Pays des Coteaux de l'Ardèche*.)

Vin de Pays de la Drome, Vin de Pays de Vaucluse, Collines Rhodaniennes, Comté de Grignan, Coteaux de Baronnies All make red, dry white and rosé wine.

name Listel, is leading experimentation into new methods of planting and wine production. Listel make both single-grape-variety wines and blends in red, dry white and *gris* rosé wine styles, as well as sparkling wine made by the Charmat method.

Vin de Pays de L'Hérault A massive production of red, dry white and rosé wines mostly from *Caves Co-opératives*. Within this *Vin de Pays* are many smaller zonal *Vin de Pays*. The following produce only red and rosé wines: Ardaillon, Bénovie, Cassan, Cessenon, Coteaux de Murviel, Coteaux de Peyriac, Coteaux du Salagou, Côtes de Brian, and Haute Vallée de l'Orb.

These produce red, white and rosé wines: Bérange, Bessans, Caux, Collines de la Moure, Coteaux d'Enserune, Coteaux de Fontcaude, Coteaux de Laurens, Coteaux de Libron, Coteaux de Céresscu, Côtes de Thau, Côtes de Thongue, Gorges de l'Hérault, Littoral Orb-Hérault, Mont Baudile, Monts de la Grage, Pézanas, Val de Montferrand and Vicomté d'Aumelas.

VINS DOUX NATURELS
Vin Doux Naturel is not wine but fortified grape juice. The grape juice must have a natural sugar content which, if fermented, would result in an alcohol concentration of 14°. The fermentation is initiated and allowed to proceed to a level of about 7° of alcohol. It is then arrested by the addition of 6-10 per cent by volume of grape alcohol at 90°. This alcohol

addition (called *mutage*) stops fermentation by killing the yeasts. The resulting product is a sweet beverage of about 21° of alcohol.

The *Vins Doux Naturels* of Languedoc are richer, more alcoholic and less aromatic than the famous Muscat-de-Beaumes-de-Venise *Vin Doux Naturel* of the Rhône Valley.

Muscat de Lunel and Muscat de Mireval White only, from the Muscat grape.

Muscat de Frontignan The best of the Languedoc white *Vin Doux Naturel*.

Muscat de Saint-Jean-de-Minervois

PROVENCE

This is a region famous for its rosé wine. It is exquisitely refreshing in the heat of the Mediterranean sun, but is somewhat lost in other climates.

APPELLATIONS CONTRÔLÉES
Palette A tiny area with one major producer, Château Simone. Red, dry white and rosé wines are made, all of which are expensive and need some ageing.

Bandol Coastal appellation producing red, dry white and rosé wine. The best is the red wine which can be very well made and quite expensive. The best estates, Domaine Tempier and Château Vannières, produce wines that need laying down for at least five years.

Cassis Red, dry white and rosé wines are produced here immediately to the east of

Marseille. The white is an excellent accompaniment to the local fish and *bouillabaisse* (fish soup).

Bellet A very small appellation near Nice producing red and white wine. The best estate is Château de Crémat, making a rich, tannic, oak-aged red wine and a white with a scent of wild flowers.

Côtes de Provence A large area producing red, dry white and rosé wines. The rosés are the best known but now the red wines may be made with up to 60 per cent Cabernet Sauvignon, which radically alters the Provence style but produces finer wines. This became *appellation contrôlée* in 1977 and the quality varies from good ordinary to quite good.

Coteaux d'Aix-en-Provence and Coteaux des Baux-en-Provence Both are satellite vineyards of Côtes de Provence, making similar red, dry white and rosé wines. Both were promoted to *appellation contrôlée* in 1986 and are excellent value.

VDQS
Coteaux de Pierrevert A smaller production of red, dry white and rosé wines, again similar to Côtes de Provence.

VIN DE PAYS
Vin de Pays des Alpes-de-Haute-Provence, Vin de Pays des Alpes-Maritimes, Vin de Pays des Bouches-du-Rhône, Vin de Pays du Var, Argens, Coteaux Varois, Maures Red, white and rosé wine.

Mont Caume Red and rosé only.

Petite Crau Red, dry white and rosé.

ADDRESSES
Palette:
M. Rougier, Château Simone, Meyreuil, Bouches-du-Rhône

Bandol:
Domaine Tempier, Château de Vannières, La Cadière d'Azur, Var

Grapes being loaded into the presses at a modern cave coopérative *near the village of Lirac in the southern Rhône*

Bellet:
Jean Bagnis, Château de
Crémat, 06200 Bellet-de-Nice

Coteaux d'Aix en Provence:
Château Vignelaure, Rians

Côtes de Provence:
Les Maitres Vignerons de la
Presqu'Ile de St Tropez.

SAVOIE

Although this is an area of great
gastronomy and spectacular
scenery, few of the wines are
good enough to sell well outside
the region. The delightful
vermouth *apéritif* Chambéry
comes from here. Its flowery
delicacy and flavour make it
distinctly superior to its Italian
counterparts.

APPELLATIONS CONTRÔLÉES
Crépy This appellation produces
dry white wines that are faintly
sparkling (*perlant* or *pétillant*).
These low-alcohol wines from
Chasselas grapes are refreshing
but not of great interest.

Roussette de Savoie This
appellation produces only white
wine from the Altesse and
Chardonnay grapes
(Chardonnay is known locally as

the Petite-Sainte-Marie) with
Mondeuse varieties. The wine is
very dry and has some finesse. It
is an excellent accompaniment
to the local freshwater fish.

This *appellation controlée* also
has individual *Crus* which are
communes that may add their
own name, but little is seen of
them outside their district.

Seyssel Dry white wines and a
particularly good *mousseux*. The
wine is light and perfumed with
a floral bouquet.

Vin de Savoie This produces red,
dry white and rosé wines that
should be drunk young. The
white wines are the best. Like
Rousette de Savoie, there are

several communes that have
been allowed since 1973 to add
their own names, for example,
Chautagne and Ripaille.

White and rosé *mousseux* is also
produced as well as a non-
appellation sparkling wine made
from wines bought in from
outside the district.

Vin de Savoie Ayze Mousseux A
similar appellation.

VDQS
Vin de Bugey A tiny but growing
production of red, dry white
(Chardonnays are especially
good) and rosé. *Mousseux* and
pétillant are also made.

VIN DE PAYS
Balmes Dauphinoises Red, dry
white and rosé of which the
white wines are best.

Coteaux du Grésivaudan Similar to
Balmes Dauphinoises.

Franche-Comté

Vin de Pays de l'Ain A tiny
production of what would
otherwise be Vin de Bugey.

ADDRESSES
Varichon et Clerc, Château des
Sechallets, 014120 Seyssel, Ain

Museums and Châteaux

When opening times are not stated it would be advisable to phone before starting out.

SAVOIE

COMITÉ INTERPROFESSIONEL DES VINS DE SAVOIE

The region's winemakers' association provides information on all the wines of Savoie, the Routes des Vins and growers to visit.
3 Rue du Château, 73000 Chambéry.
Tel (79) 33–44–16.

CAVEAU BUGISTE

Co-operative in handsome old buildings at Vongnes in *vin de Bugey* country. The wines made here are humble *vins de pays*, but quality is consistently high. Visitors see a delightful little wine museum, and taste the co-operative's range in a charming, rustic *caveau de dégustation*.
Vongnes, 01350 Culoz.
Tel (79) 87–92–37.
Open daily, 3–7pm.

CO-OPÉRATIVE DE VENTE DES VINS FINS DE SAVOIE

Visitors can tour the cellars and taste the wines from the large selection offered at this major co-operative. Prices are keen, and there is a notably – and unusually – good choice of half bottles on sale.
Rue Antoine Besson, 73800 Montmélian.
Tel (79) 65–22–01.
Open Tue–Sat, 8am–12 noon and 2–6pm.

FICHARD

At Crépy in the Haute Savoie, Fichard is one of the top-rated winemakers. Visitors are welcome to tour the winery, and the wines can be tasted and purchased. At Chens on the eastern shore of Lake Geneva.
Chens-sur-Léman, 74140 Douvaine.
Tel (50) 94–04–02.
Open Mon–Fri, by appointment only.

LA TOUR DE MARIGNAN

At Marignan in the Haute Savoie, the region's northern end, this small estate produces only 15,000 bottles of wine – dry white, and some sparkling – annually. The vineyard surrounds an ancient fortified house, complete with massive tower, built around the year 1000. Owner Bernard Canelli-Suchet will happily show visitors round and offers tastings.
Marignan, 74140 Sciez.
Tel (50) 72–60–05.
Open daily, but telephone for an appointment.

LE VIGNERON SAVOYARD

Small-scale co-operative in the village of Apremont, with its own *caveau de dégustation-vente*. Fine wines on sale at alluring prices.
Apremont, 73190 Challes-les-Eaux.
Tel (79) 28–33–23.
Open Mon–Fri, 9am–12 noon and 2–6pm.

VIGNOBLES DUPASQUIER D'AIMAVIGNE

The Dupasquier family have made wine at Aimavigne, a scenic vineyard close to the village of Jonquieux, for four generations. Visitors are welcome to see over the winery and taste its fruits.
Aimavigne, 73170 Jongieux.
Tel (79) 44–02–23.
It is vital to telephone first.

RHONE

MAISON DU TOURISME ET DU VIN

Provides information on touring the region and visiting vineyards throughout the Rhône Valley. An indispensable starting point for visitors. In Avignon in the southern Rhône.
41 Cours Jean-Jaurès, Avignon, 84000 Vaucluse.
Tel (90) 82-65-11.
Open office hours, year-round.

CAVES DES VIGNERONS DE BEAUMES-DE-VENISE

The co-operative in this idyllic village – now so well known for its luscious dessert wines (*vins doux naturels*) made from the Muscat grape – makes some of the best wines of the appellation. Visitors see the *caves* and can taste the wines.
84190 Beaumes-de-Venise.
Tel (90) 62–94–45.
Open Mon to Sat, 8am–12 noon and 2–6pm.

GEORGES VERNAY & FILS

On the N 86 road through Condrieu in the northern Rhône, the rather forbidding villa and winery of the Condrieu appellation's largest estate is conspicuously marked out by a gigantic *papier mâché* bottle

The ochre-tinted village of Roussillon perched on the brink of sandstone cliffs in the Vaucluse

emblazoned with the word 'Viognier' – the grape that has made the fortune of Monsieur Vernay and the trendy dry white wine he has almost single-handedly brought to worldwide fame. Visitors are welcome to taste and buy.
69420 Condrieu.
Open Mon–Sat, 9am–12 noon and 2–6pm.

PAUL JABOULET AÎNÉ

One of the famous names of the revered Hermitage hillside vineyards – producing outstanding red and white wines. The cellars here are said to hold half a million bottles.
Les Jalets, RN7, 46 La Roche-de-Glun, 26600 Tain-l'Hermitage.
Tel (75) 84–68–93.
Open Mon–Fri 8am–12 noon and 1.30–6.30pm. Closed August.

PÈRE ANSELME

In the village of Châteauneuf-du-Pape, many famous firms have their *caves* and tasting rooms. Père Anselme upstages all of them by incorporating a remarkable *musée du vin* in its 300-year-old premises on the Avignon road. Well worth a visit – and the wines are worthy of tasting, too.
84230 Châteauneuf-du-Pape.
Tel (90) 83–51–64.
Open daily, 8am–12 noon and 2–6pm.

LANGUEDOC

MUSÉE DE LA VIGNE ET DU VIN, LEZIGNAN-CORBIÈRES

The museum has historic and colourful exhibitions of every stage of the vineyard year:

ploughing and pruning, picking and pressing as well as winemaking itself. A quick tour gives a good impression of just what a laborious task winemaking in the heat of the Languedoc has always been.

In the charming adjacent stable buildings there is a tempting shop where you can taste and buy all kinds of Languedoc wines and spirits, and local gastronomic specialities such as *cassoulet*, cured meats, Corbières goat's cheese and honey. The museum is opposite the railway station.
11200 Lezignan-Corbières.
Tel (68) 27–07–57.
Open daily, 9am–12 noon and 2–7pm.

CHÂTEAU DE GREZAN

On the site of a great Roman villa at Faugères, the spectacular château with its numerous *chais* (above-ground cellars) enclosed within a complete castellated and turreted medieval wall dates from the twelfth century. You can taste and buy the excellent wines made here – and be shown around on request.
Laurens, 34480 Magalas.
Tel (67) 90–28–03.
Telephone to arrange a visit.

CHÂTEAU DES LASTOURS

Modern winery set on a plateau a thousand feet up in the hills overlooking the Mediterranean. Tours of the *chais* – which double as galleries of art and sculpture – and tastings of the first-rank Corbières wines.
11490 Porrel des Corbières.
Tel (68) 48–29–17.
Telephone to check opening times.

The seventeenth-century château of Entrecasteaux in the Var

DOMAINE DES JOUGLA

André and Alain Jougla welcome visitors to their St Chinian property and will show you round the winery as well as offering tastings of their wines.
Prades-sur-Vernazobre, 34360 Saint-Chinian.
Tel (67) 38–06–02.
Telephone for an appointment.

MAS DE DAUMAS GASSAC

This is a shrine for wine-lovers – the home of the greatest wines of the Languedoc region. Owners Aimé and Véronique Gilbert receive as many as 3,000 visitors each season; they see over the modern winery which produces classic, Bordeaux-like red wine and fine dry white in the style of Condrieu. The first of these phenomenal wines went on sale in 1981, but the property already has an international reputation. Tastings are offered, and you can buy mature vintages which are extremely rare outside France.
Routeau Capion, Aniane, 34150 Gignac.
Tel (67) 57–71–28.
Open Jun 15–Sep 15, 10am–12 noon and 2–6pm except Sun and holidays; Sat only for the rest of the year. Closed Jan and Feb. Wine shop open Mon–Fri 2–6pm all year.

accommodate the making of the delicate *appellation contrôlée* Bellet wines of the estate's present owner Charles Bagnis.
Château Bagnis, 442 Chemin de Crémat, 06200 Nice.
Tel (93) 37–80–30.
Telephone for appointment and directions.

CHÂTEAU SIMONE

East of Aix-en-Provence, this stately mansion looms imperiously over its vineyards – arranged in classical symmetry beyond its elegant fringe of terraces, parterres and water gardens. Simone occupies two-thirds of the entire Palette *appellation contrôlée* district – which is, it must be said, one of the very smallest *appellations contrôlées* in France. You can taste and buy the fine red, white and rosé wines made here.
13590 Meyreuil.
Tel (42) 28–92–58.
Open Mon–Sat 8am–12 noon and 2–6pm.

PROVENCE

MAISON DES VINS CÔTES DE PROVENCE

Information on touring the region, visiting vineyards and buying wine in Provence. A useful starting point.
3 Avenue de la Gare, Les Arcs, 83460 Var.
Tel (94) 73–37–30.
Open office hours June–September.

CHÂTEAU LA CANORGUE

The sublime Provençal château, built where a Roman villa once stood, produces an appropriately lovely red wine and an exceptional dry white under the Côtes du Lubéron appellation. Owner Jean-Pierre Margan proudly shows visitors

around the newly restored winery, and offers tastings.
84480 Bonnieux.
Tel (90) 75–81–01.
Open Mon–Sat, 9am–12 noon and 3–7pm.

CHÂTEAU DE CRÉMAT

In the hills behind Nice, a curious mock-Camelot of a castle built in the last century over ancient cellars excavated by the Romans. The ancient diggings are put to good use to

MAS DE LA ROUVIÈRE

Mas is the old Provence word for farmhouse, and the wine made under this name by the Bunan family is so-called after the old house among the vines at Le Castellet in the dreamy hinterland back of Bandol – the fashionable seaside resort down the road. Tasting the magnificent reds, rosés and whites of Rouvière is an experience not to be missed.
Le Castellet, 83330 Le Beausset.
Tel (94) 98–72–76.
Open Mon–Sat 8am–12 noon and 2–6pm.

Gastronomic Specialities

SAVOIE

SAVOYARD on a menu usually signifies a dish made with the Gruyère-type cheeses of the region.

SOUPE SAVOYARDE is a hearty wintertime soup based on onions, leeks, potatoes, turnip and celery with milk added towards the end of the cooking. *Croutes* (small slices of bread fried in butter) topped with slices of cheese are added just before serving.

GRATIN SAVOYARD is a simple, but delicious potato and cheese dish. The potatoes are thinly sliced and arranged in a baking dish in layers – each layer seasoned with salt, pepper and nutmeg then sprinkled with grated cheese. A mildly flavoured broth is added to keep it moist.

SANGLIER is wild boar – one of several game meats that are a feature of menus here in the heart of France's Alpine hunting country. CHEVREUIL (venison) and LIÈVRE (hare) also make frequent appearances in strong-flavoured stews and *ragouts* that make these exotic meats agreeably tender.

OMBLE CHEVALIER is the most-prized of the rich variety of freshwater fish taken from Savoie's vast Lac du Bourget. It is a beautifully flavoured variety

Left: A small épicerie *in the wine village of Tain l'Hermitage near Tournon in the northern Rhône valley*

of trout – weighing up to 30 pounds.

COMTÉ is perhaps the best known of the hard cheeses of the region that are made in the style of the Gruyère from across the border in Switzerland. BEAUFORT is similar, but without holes. TOMME DE SAVOIE is softer, with a fine, nutty aroma. BLEU DE GEX is a blue-veined cheese, and REBLOCHON a medium-soft variety made in small discs – one of the most delicious cheeses in France.

THE RHONE

Lyon, standing at the head of the Rhône Valley, styles itself the gastronomic capital of France. The city teems with fine restaurants, and there are countless shops offering the exotic local specialities:

CHARCUTERIE Among the great sausages of the region, ROSETTE DE LYON, a salami-style pork variety ranks the most famous; SAUCISSON A L'AIL is a garlic sausage sold either cooked or uncooked (the latter is not suitable for taking home if your journey will be more than a few miles!). ANDOUILLETTES LYONNAISES are delicious veal-tripe sausages for frying.

DAUBE A stew – most commonly of beef, sometimes of lamb – cooked in wine, garlic, tomatoes and herbs that occurs in different variations all over southern France. Traditionally, it is cooked for many hours, concentrating the sauce into a flavoursome, richly dense texture.

QUENELLES One of the great specialities of Lyon, these are little balls or dumplings of pounded pike flesh. Restaurants vie with each other to make the lightest possible *quenelles* – to the point where this admirable delicacy can become too light in weight and flavour to be enjoyable.

GRATINÉE LYONNAISE is very much a down-to-earth, bistro dish. It is onion soup topped with a cap of toast and grilled cheese. A lavish variation is to add a glass of port mixed with egg yolk immediately before serving.

GÂTEAU LYONNAIS is a wonderful confection of chocolate and chestnut purée – very rich, and often decorated with elaborate chocolate ornamentation. One of many chocolate specialities of Lyon.

PROVENCE

SAUCE PROVENÇALE sums up the horticultural armoury of a region that has retained its culinary traditions in spite of a century of annually accelerating tourist invasions: garlic and tomatoes, olive oil and wine, a host of herbs. These essential ingredients of the 'Mediterranean diet' – said to be one of the healthiest in the world – pervade Provence's many famous specialities.

RATATOUILLE celebrates the region's great success at growing and cooking with vegetables. Aubergines, courgettes, onions, red or green peppers and, of course, garlic

A rural landscape near Vidauban with the Massifs des Maures visible in the background

and tomatoes are all essential. Herbs such as basil, thyme and sage are added, with coriander and aniseed for spice. The prepared ingredients are cooked in a good measure of olive oil.

SOUPE DE POISSONS PROVENÇALE Fish figures larger than meat in the southern diet, even though supplies from the Mediterranean are dwindling from the effects of severe pollution. In the smart resort hotels, the ingredients for many a fish dish are now bought in from Atlantic ports. Provençale fish soup is based either on white fish or mussels – puréed to a rich consistency and flavoured with fennel, garlic,

tomatoes and perhaps *anise* liquor (eg Pernod).

BOUILLABAISSE The celebrated fish stew is made very much according to the ingredients at hand, but will always include several varieties of firm, white fish and shellfish fried in olive oil with garlic, onions and

saffron, then cooked in their own stock.

LOUP DE MER 'Sea wolf' is in fact sea bass – a favourite, if costly, item on Provençale menus. The fish is at its best simply baked, perhaps with a stick of fennel inside for flavour. Some restaurants serve *loup* flambéd in Pernod.

PISSALADIÈRE is a reminder that Italy is just along the coast for it is, in effect, pizza. Olives, anchovies, onions and tomatoes are baked on a bread of yeast dough.

PISTOU is a delicious paste of basil, garlic and parmesan

assembled with the haricot beans, garlic, onions and tomatoes for the final baking.

CAILLETTES DE LANGUEDOC are flavoursome cakes of sausage meat based on pork and pork liver – with garlic and onions and a mixture of herbs including sage, thyme and bay leaf.

BOURRIDE is Languedoc's answer to *bouillabaisse* (though you will certainly find *bouillabaisse* itself listed on Languedoc menus). It is a rich fish soup flavoured with garlic, onion and herbs, but leaving out the tomatoes and saffron that characterise its famous cousin.

MORUE MINERVOISE is a dish based on dried salt cod cooked in Minervois wine with onions and garlic, olives and anchovies.

COURGETTES FARCIES Vegetables thrive here as they do in Provence, and many crops – aubergines and tomatoes as well as courgettes – are ideal for serving *farcie* (stuffed with minced beef, pork or chicken, cooked rice, egg and garlic) as a simple main dish.

ROQUEFORT The famous blue cheese from ewe's milk comes from Roquefort-sur-Soulzon in the northern Languedoc. The exclusive right to make cheese under this name has belonged to Roquefort since the granting of a special royal warrant in 1411. It is expensive, but may well deserve its reputation as the best cheese in the world.

cheese – again, a close relative of an Italian speciality, *pesto*. Pistou is stirred into soup or served with pasta, or used as a pungent dip for *crudités* (sliced raw vegetables).

AÏOLI is Provence's own powerfully aromatic garlic mayonnaise. It is served with fish, meat and salad dishes, and even added to fish soups. The name *aïoli* is also given to a dish consisting of salt cod, hard-boiled eggs and squid, plus potatoes, carrots and beans – all served with the garlic mayonnaise itself.

ROUILLE is a relative of *aïoli* – a garlicky sauce spiked with chili peppers. It is stirred into fish soups.

LANGUEDOC

CASSOULET DE TOULOUSE enjoys a reputation as the richest of the regional variations on the theme of the hearty haricot bean and meat casserole that takes its name from the deep, earthenware *cassoulet* pot in which this great dish is made. The Toulouse version calls for *confits* (pieces of meat long-preserved in their own fat) of duck or goose as well as bacon, lamb and succulent Toulouse pork sausages in the recipe. These are all separately prepared and cooked, then

Hotels and Restaurants

SAVOIE

AUBERGE GOURMANDE

A large restaurant in the vineyards of Crépy, it has five excellent set menus at a wide range of prices. The dining room is surprisingly cosy in winter, warmed by a roaring fire, and there is a fine terrace for summer meals with good views of the Jura mountains. Specialities include a salad of artichokes with *foie gras* and turbot in a cream and lentil sauce. Closed for ten days in Feb and in Nov, according to school holidays.
74140 Massongy Douvaine.
Tel (50) 94–16–97.

LE BATEAU IVRE

Waterside restaurant on Savoie's Lac du Bourget, housed in an old – but beautifully converted – store for the local salt. Fish from the lake are very much a speciality and the cooking is of the highest standard (two stars in the Michelin Guide). Closed Nov to end Apr, and on Tue.
73370 Le Bourget du Lac.
Tel (79) 25–02–66.

CHÂTEAU DE COLLONGES

A *chic* hotel with nine rooms – each exquisitely decorated and furnished – this converted country château stands in its own delightful parkland, complete with swimming pool. The restaurant is stylish, and the cooking good if unexciting.

Left: A café in the charming small square of Roussillon in the Vaucluse

Closed Jan 5 to Feb 8. Restaurant closed Mon lunchtime and all day Tue.
Ruffieux, 73310 Chindrieux.
Tel (79) 54–27–38.

HÔTEL LES PRINCES

Medium-sized hotel (45 rooms) close to the centre of Chambéry – functional and comfortable and very reasonably priced. The restaurant enjoys a good reputation for its fish dishes.
4 Rue de Boigne, Chambéry, 73000 Savoie.
Tel (79) 33–45–36.

HÔTEL DU RHÔNE

Appropriately named – it stands on the right bank of the Rhône river at Seyssel – this is an old-fashioned hotel with a friendly atmosphere to make up for the lack of modern amenities. There are 15 rooms. The restaurant is small, but the cooking aspires to great things. Specialities such as *poularde de Bresse aux morilles* (chicken with wild mushrooms) have won the place a star in the Michelin Guide.
01420 Seyssel.
Tel (50) 59–20–30.

RHONE

AUBERGE DE TAVEL

Highly rated restaurant with rooms in the village at the centre of Rhône rosé country. The menu includes a good choice of fresh fish dishes with which to enjoy the delightful pink wines. Closed Nov 3 to Dec 15 and Jan 15 to Mar 15. Restaurant closed Mon except in Jul and Aug.
Voie Romaine, 30126 Tavel.
Tel (66) 50–03–41.

LA BEAUGRAVIÈRE

Owner Guy Jullien makes a great speciality of truffles at this nevertheless inexpensive and charming restaurant. The kitchen is a feature of the place – as you must pass through it to get to the dining room! There is a very pleasant and shady terrace where meals are served in the warmer months, and there are seven bedrooms. Highly recommended. Closed Sep 15 to 30 and Sun evening.
Route Nationale 7, 84430 Mondragon.
Tel (90) 40–82–54.

HOSTELLERIE LES FLORETS

Tranquil hotel-restaurant in the heart of the revered Côtes du Rhône vineyard of Gigondas. Meals are served on a large and leafy terrace as well as in the comfortable dining room. Specialities include a sublime stew of fresh tuna made with Gigondas wine. Closed Jan and Feb and on Wed.
84190 Gigondas.
Tel (90) 65–85–01.

HÔTEL DU CHÂTEAU

On the Rhône quayside at Tournon, a hotel with 'a unique view on to the slopes of the Hermitage' – that is, of the vineyards where Hermitage, the Rhône Valley's most revered red wine, is made. The restaurant specialises in dishes with which to sample the extensive list of costly Hermitages. There are 29 spacious rooms. Closed Nov 1 to 15 and Feb 1 to 15.
12 Quai Marc Seguin, 07300 Tournon.
Tel (75) 08–60–22.

LA MULE-DU-PAPE

An upstairs restaurant in the
centre of Châteauneuf-du-Pape,
in bright Provençale style.
There are good local specialities
and, of course, plenty of fine
Châteauneuf wines to try. The
curious name of the place is
taken from the mules upon
which the Avignon popes would
ride to their new home
(*châteauneuf* means new castle)
to inspect its construction.
Closed Mon evening and all
Tue.
*Place de la Fontaine, 84230
Châteauneuf-du-Pape.
Tel (90) 39–73–30.*

PROVENCE

AUBERGE DU VIEUX FOUR

In the centre of the resort town
of Fréjus, a small hotel (eight
rooms) with an excellent
restaurant offering Provence
specialities and a very good
wine list. Closed Oct 25 to Nov
15, and Sun evenings and Wed
out of season.
*57 Rue Grisolle, 83600 Fréjus.
Tel (94) 51–56–38.*

AUBERGE PROVENÇALE

Devotees of this attractive and
simple restaurant heap special
praise on the *hors d'oeuvre*.
Classic Provençale cookery at
affordable prices. Closed Nov,
Feb, and Thu lunch.
*13180 Eygalières.
Tel (90) 95–91–00.*

LE CHABICHOU

Very smart St Tropez
restaurant whose wonderful
choice of fish dishes and epic

prices are very nearly
overshadowed by the antics of
the voguish local *clientele*. Well
worth it for the food – and the
sights. Closed Oct to end Apr.
*Avenue Foch, 83990 St Tropez.
Tel (94) 54–80–00.*

HOSTELLERIE BÉRARD

In La Cadière, an ancient
hilltop village behind Bandol,
this smart hotel has spectacular
views, and every comfort
including excellent food and
wine. It is the preferred retreat
of Formula One racing drivers
from the nearby Paul Ricard
circuit during the annual Grand
Prix. Closed Jan.
*83740 La Cadière-d'Azur.
Tel (94) 90–11–43.*

HOSTELLERIE DU CÔTEAU FLEURIE

Small (14 rooms), picturesque
hotel with lovely valley views
from Grimaud. Good restaurant
and very modest prices. Hotel
closed Nov and Feb; restaurant
closed mid-Oct to mid-May and
on Wed except in high season.
*83360 Grimaud.
Tel (94) 43–20–17.*

The tiny square of Villeneuvette, an industrial village established in the seventeenth century near Clermont-l'Herault

LANGUEDOC

CHÂTEAU DE VIOLET

Château hotel with 16 rooms, all lavishly furnished, idyllically set in its own park in Minervois wine country. Duck dishes are a speciality of the comfortable dining room – ideal accompaniments to the robust red wines of the region. Closed Oct to end May.
11160 Peyriac–Minervois.
Tel (68) 78–10–42.

CAVE D'AGNES

Simple village restaurant serving local specialities – and the hearty local Fitou wine – at very fair prices. Closed Oct to mid-Mar.
11510 Fitou. Tel (68) 45–75–91.

LE LANGUEDOC

Cassoulet au confit de canard, a great speciality of the region, is among the delicious local dishes at this well-priced restaurant, charmingly built around a central courtyard. Closed Dec 15 to Jan 15 and on Mon.
32 Allée d'Iéna, 11000 Carcassonne.
Tel (68) 25–22–17.

RELAIS CHANTOVENT

Charmingly situated restaurant with five rooms at Minèrve – the village from which Minervois wines take their name. Food is delicious and inexpensive. Closed Jan 5 to end Feb and on Mon except in Jul and Aug.
34120 Minèrve.
Tel (68) 91–22–96.

RELAIS DU VAL D'ORBIEU

A conversion of an old mill has made for a very comfortable and peaceful 25-room hotel here in the heart of the Corbières vineyards. There is a large garden, swimming pool and smart restaurant. Open all year.
11200 Ornaisons (on the route départmentale *24).*
Tel (68) 27–10–27.

Calendar of Events

JANUARY

Beginning of the month – Wine competition of the Aude in Carcassonne (Aude)

Weekend in middle of month – Competition for tasting new wines in Orange (Vaucluse)

Sunday nearest 22nd – Wine market in Ampuis (Rhône)

FEBRUARY

Beginning of the month – Fête du Raisin in Valbonne (Alpes Maritimes)

MARCH

Weekend a fortnight before Easter – Wine exhibition in Vinsobres (Drôme)

APRIL

Côtes du Rhône Gardoise Wine Fair in Villeneuve-lès-Avignon (Gard)

Middle of the month – Var and Provence wine festival in Brignoles (Var)

End of the month – Spring wine fair in Narbonne (Aude)

25th – Festival of St Mark in Châteauneuf-du-Pape (Vaucluse)

Last Sunday – Festival of St Vincent in Tavel (Gard)

MAY

Festival of Côtes du Rhône wines in Vacqueyras (Vaucluse)

Ascension – *Vins de Pays* festival in Roquemaure (Gard)

JUNE

June – Cherry festival in Caromb (Vaucluse)

Middle of the month – Côtes de Provence wine festival in Le Thoronet (Var)

Middle of the month – Côtes de Provence wine festival in St Raphaël (Var)

JULY

1st fortnight – Wine festival in Trausse Minervois (Aude)

2nd fortnight – Wine and local products festival in Minerve (Hérault)

3rd week – Wine fair in Buisson (Rhône)

JULY AND AUGUST

Permanent wine exhibition in the amphitheatre grotto in Orange (Vaucluse)

AUGUST

Summer feast in Caromb (Vaucluse)

Lac du Bourget seen from the promenade at Aix-les-Bains

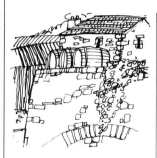

1st Sunday – vine festival in Nice (Alpes Maritimes)

1st fortnight – Wine festival in Lézignan (Aude)

1st fortnight – Great wine festival in Saissac (Aude)

2nd weekend – Wine fair in St Antonin (Var)

Weekend of 15th – Great wine festival in Stade Sigean (Aude)

Weekend of 15th – Feria de Béziers (Wine fountain) in Béziers (Hérault)

2nd weekend – Wine and vine festival in Fréjus (Var)

2nd fortnight – Wine festival in Lagrasse (Aude)

2nd fortnight – Wine and local products festival in Minerve (Hérault)

Middle of the month – Wine fairs in Séguret (Vaucluse)

4th weekend – Vine festival in Le Plan de La Tour (Var)

4th weekend – Wine and vine festival in Ste Maxime (Var)

SEPTEMBER

Harvest festival in La Cadière d'Azur (Var)

Festival of St Maurice in Caromb (Vaucluse)

1st weekend – Harvest festival in Grimaud (Var)

1st weekend – Wine festival in St Péray (Ardèche)

1st fortnight – Wine festival in Bram (Aude)

Middle of the month – Harvest festival in St Tropez (Var)

3rd weekend – Harvest festival in Bormes-les-Mimosas (Var)

3rd weekend – Announcement of the harvest in Châteauneuf-du-Pape (Vaucluse)

3rd weekend – Harvest festival in Tain l'Hermitage (Drôme)

3rd weekend – Harvest festival in Taradeau (Var)

End of the month – Corrida des Vendanges in Arles (Bouches-du-Rhône)

Last Sunday – Corrida des vendanges in Nîmes (Gard)

OCTOBER

2nd fortnight – International wine and vine fair in Montpellier (Hérault)

3rd Sunday – New wine fair in Béziers (Hérault)

NOVEMBER

Beginning of the month – Côtes du Rhône competition in Vaison-la-Romaine (Vaucluse)

DECEMBER

1st Sunday – Wine fair in Cornas (Ardèche)

Index

INDEX